25+ NEW JEWELRY DESIGNS

TWO-HOLE
Bead Stitching

Kalmbach
Media

VIRGINIA JENSEN

Kalmbach Media
21027 Crossroads Circle
Waukesha, Wisconsin 53186
www.JewelryAndBeadingStore.com

Published in 2019
23 22 21 20 19   2 3 4 5 6

Manufactured in China

ISBN: 978-1-62700-616-3
EISBN: 978-1-62700-617-0

Editor: Erica Barse
Development Editor: Dianne Wheeler
Book Design: Lisa Bergman
Photographer: William Zuback

Library of Congress Control Number: 2018965245

Contents

Introduction

Two-hole beads have exploded! There seems to be a new shape every week, and now the number of holes have multiplied too, with three- and four-hole beads. Some beaders may find the greatly expanded selection overwhelming. I agree it is a lot to wade through, with many decisions to make, especially if you are a hobbyist or part-time beader.

Of course, the stitches all have to be rewritten to accommodate the two holes, and that was the purpose of my last book. As I worked further, I found that certain stitches translated easily into two-hole use. But I also created several new stitches that these new beads evoked. I'm sure the three- and four-hole beads will generate more new forms and stitches to make use of their unique qualities as well.

I've tried to start each chapter with an easy piece and then moved on to more intermediate and difficult designs, but sometimes the easy-to-hard order is not as simple as it may seem. If you're a beginner, there will be plenty of easy pieces and basic techniques for you to learn.

I've included a section of earrings. If you're a longtime beader, you will have lots of extra beads from larger projects. I love to find uses for these. And, I love to wear earrings.

I know when I open a beadwork book, I want to make the first thing that catches my eye. Often that's one of the more difficult pieces. However, take the time to make a simple version with the same stitch. It makes doing the difficult piece much easier.

There are so many two-hole beads, I have not been able to use all of them. However, that leaves a lot of room for you to experiment. I give you options when I see where it is easy to substitute one two-hole bead for another. I'm sure some of you will take off on creative urges of your own, and I wish you all well.

Happy beading!
— Virginia

Basics

TOOLS

My tools have not changed substantially over many years. I still love my #10 beading needle and 8- or 10-lb. Power Pro. But I always encourage beaders to work with what suits them and makes a sound and attractive piece of work.

Your thread should be flexible, strong, non-stretch, and if possible, braided (so it's harder to split and catch). I use 8-lb. Power Pro for earrings and fine work, and I switch to 10-lb. for necklaces and heavy bracelets. Fireline is an alternative when I need black. If I need to color-match, I will use C-Lon or something similar.

I've tried different needles and will switch to #11 or #12 if needed, but I find my hand works best with the standard #10. Any finer needles, and I find myself bending them into unusable shapes. With my sturdy #10s, I just take the pliers and straighten them a bit, and I'm back in business.

You'll need a place to lay out your beads, such as a felt mat, sticky mat, or bowls. I prefer my little white oriental dipping bowls. It's easy to move the beads around en masse and I can pick up the beads without catching the tip of the needle. They require less contortion of the hand, and when I'm finished, it's easy to pour the beads into my hand and back into their home containers.

Other necessities include: scissors that cut cleanly and closely, a couple of fine pliers, a ruler (preferably with millimeter markings), some kind of magnifier (you're bound to need it eventually), and finally, good light.

Make friends with your ophthalmologist if you have any kind of problem seeing your work. I've solved a couple of problems with just a lens correction or a different pair of glasses more suited to beadwork.

TECHNIQUES

My experience teaching has made me realize how important a bit of preparatory work can be when learning to bead. It's hard enough for some people to learn a stitch, and it can be much harder when they are still trying to learn how to manage thread and needle.

By starting with some of the easy pieces in this book, the beginner can become familiar with the tricks thread will play on you—and they are many and varied. I may spend more time in class helping beginners untangle thread than anything else. Take your time, and you'll be glad you did later, when you're able to whizz through a piece and untie the most frustrating knots. My trick: insert two needles from opposite sides into the heart of the knot and wiggle until something gives. The three areas that most puzzled me when I began beading were adding thread, ending thread, and attaching clasps, so I've addressed them here.

Adding Thread

Just take your thread back into the piece a few beads (or about a half inch), until it won't easily pull back out. Start the new thread as if running continuously from where the old thread ended, and leave a tail long enough to tie to the old thread (about 6 in./15 cm). Work your way back to exit exactly where you were with the old thread. Tie the two ends together with a **surgeon's knot**.

SURGEON'S KNOT

This process is much like working a maze. You may have to try several routes in your mind before finding the one that will be least visible. Practice will make this much easier. It helps if you plan this juncture to occur next to a bead that has a hole big enough to pull the knot into. I use a surgeon's knot, but if you have very small holes, use an **overhand knot**, as it's less bulky. After you tie the knot, take one of the ends into the nearest large hole and tug on it just a bit to get the knot to slip into the bead hole. Your knot is now hidden. Just remember not to pull so hard when finishing the other thread that you pull the knot out of the hole. Use this technique when ending threads as well.

OVERHAND KNOT

At first, I was eager to end every thread and hide the tails. Now, I may just leave the tails loose until I've finished the piece, then tie everything off at once. You never know what might happen before a piece is finished, and it's saved my work more than once to have those threads untied.

Ending Thread

Whenever possible, I like to tie two ends together using a surgeon's knot, then pull the knot into the nearest bead. Always run the tails away from the knot for about an inch in opposite directions before you cut them. I tie a **half-hitch knot** just a few beads before I cut. This prevents the tail from springing out.

HALF-HITCH KNOT

When you have only one thread ending, use several half-hitch knots spaced a few beads apart. Tie your half-hitch knot onto a crossing thread, if possible, so the knot will not slide forward when you continue beading. I sometimes tie a double half-hitch knot, one under a crossing thread and another under the same crossing thread, but starting in the opposite direction.

The best rule I know for working the thread through the work when adding or ending thread is this: you can go anywhere with the thread you've already been without it showing, but if you start adding new tracks, they are more likely to show.

Don't end a thread at the edge of the work because it will be more visible. Bury it in the middle of the work and on the underside, if there is one. Pull on the end to take up any slack right before you cut it.

Attaching Clasps

Plan the clasp you are going to use when you start your piece, and you will save yourself a lot of trouble. Some of the pieces in this book start with a doubled thread, so you can simply attach the loop to one end of a clasp or to a soldered jump ring using a **lark's head knot**.

LARK'S HEAD KNOT

I've used ready-made clasps in this book, but you can experiment with decorative clasps for your pieces.

Use toggle clasps for narrow bracelets. When using a toggle, there must be room for the bar to fold back and enter the loop, so add a few beads to equal the length of one of the arms of the bar before attaching it. If the bracelet is very narrow or if the bracelet naturally comes to a point, you will need fewer additional beads.

You can also use a magnetic clasp, especially for lightweight bracelets and necklaces. These are also useful if the wearer has difficulty fastening, such as children or those with limited motion or control. I've also found that you have to be careful with the type of jump ring you use to attach the magnetic clasps. The magnets can have quite a strong bond, and the act of pulling the sides apart may require a kind of strength that could pull open a weak jump ring. Use a soldered jump ring or be sure the gauge is adequate for the force that will be exerted on it.

Sewing on a multi-loop clasp requires a bit of planning. You can sew the ring into a bead, onto a bead, or to the thread running between beads. In the first case, you exit the bead through the ring and sew back into the bead. Turn around in the work, and repeat. In the second case, exit one side of the bead through the ring and sew back into the bead. Then sew through the other side of the bead and the ring, and sew back in.

When sewing the ring to the thread, reinforce that thread by adding passes, so that you are sewing onto a few threads, not just one.

With multiple loops (and depending on the stitch), you might have to use any or all of these options. Set the clasp against the end of the bracelet and study the fit. This determines which attachment will work best on each of the rings and allow the clasp to lay properly. Remember, you can add one or more beads to extend the attachment so the clasp sits evenly across the width of the bracelet.

Never leave an attachment hanging by a single thread. I try to make two passes at the very least, but preferably three or four. This is the part of the piece that will get the most stress as the wearer puts the piece on and takes it off.

MATERIALS

Every design in this book has a materials list. The number of beads in the list are based on the actual piece associated with the design, which is usually an average size. If you want the piece to be larger or smaller, please adjust accordingly. Because there are numerous options for adapting the designs, materials and quantities may change as you put together your piece. Refer to the the supply notes as needed.

One of the materials you might not have on hand is 3–4mm soldered jump rings. I keep these in silver and gold color plate, and use them to transition from thread to metal or wire. Never attach thread to an open jump ring. The mischievous thread will invariably find the tiny gap and slip through.

With necklaces, I like to use soldered jump rings to end the neck strand because they let me change the clasp if I want, and I can easily add an extender when necessary.

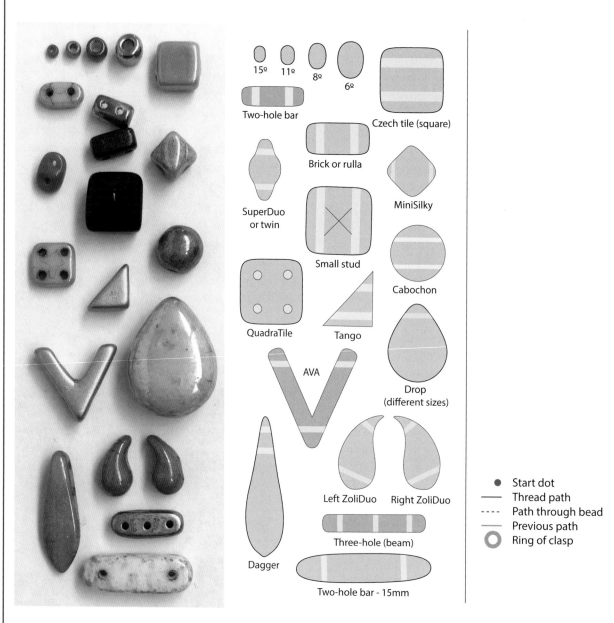

Legend:

● Start dot
— Thread path
---- Path through bead
— Previous path
⊙ Ring of clasp

Bead types: 15º, 11º, 8º, 6º, Two-hole bar, Czech tile (square), Brick or rulla, SuperDuo or twin, MiniSilky, Small stud, QuadraTile, Tango, Cabochon, AVA, Drop (different sizes), Left ZoliDuo, Right ZoliDuo, Dagger, Three-hole (beam), Two-hole bar - 15mm

A Note About Illustrations

If you're a visual learner, these illustrations will guide you through each project, step-by-step, in addition to the written instructions. Follow the order of colors as instructed. The beginning of each color is indicated with a matching colored dot, showing where to start.

These illustrated beads are not colored. I've found that using colors in the illustrations is confusing because what

is dark for the author may be light in the beader's palette. These illustrations use shading to indicate old and new beads. The beads already incorporated are lighter and the new beads are darker. I have added a bit of color when it was useful to indicate a pattern or to draw attention to a particular bead or action.

Types of Two-Hole Beads

Czech glass beads are beads made in the Czech Republic, in the particular areas of Jablonec and Nisou. Production of glass beads in these areas dates back to the 14th century (though production was depressed under communist rule). Because of this long tradition, their workmanship and quality has an excellent reputation.

For a long time, the most popular manufacturers of seed beads have been the Japanese companies Toho and Miyuki. These seed beads are first made as long, thin, hollow extrusions of glass which are then cut into tiny sections, and ground or tumbled into roundness. Then they are polished, coated or cut into the familiar round 15°, 11°, 8°, or 6° sizes.

Pressed glass beads are made differently. Just as the name sounds, they are molten glass that is pressed into the shape of tiny moulds. Moulding a bead to a tiny size as small as most seed beads is not practical, but to obtain a variety of shapes and multiple holes, pressing can provide many more options. In addition, pressing a bead allows different designs on the front and back—and there are some beads with flat backs and molded fronts.

Sources

Starman's line of multi-hole beads is called CzechMates and includes the two-hole tile, dagger, brick, lentil, triangle, bar, crescent, diamond, and cabochon; plus the three-hole beam and the four-hole QuadraTile and QuadraLentil.

Matubo produces the two-hole, diamond-shaped bead called GemDuo with a contoured side and a flat side and the Nib-Bit, a thick, trapezoidal two-hole bead.

Puca is a French jewelry designer who created several of the new shaped multi-hole beads. Arcos are arc-shaped beads with three holes; Kheops are triangular, pyramid-shaped beads with two holes; and,Tinos are trapezoidal beads with two holes. Kos is a two-hole half-disk; Paros is a two-hole, elongated hexagon that is drilled diagonally; and Amos is a petal-shaped, two-hole bead.

Potomac Bead is responsible for the StormDuo, a lightning-shaped, two-hole bead; the IrisDuo, a pointed oval with two holes; the AVA bead, a V-shaped bead with holes in the bottom and in both arms of the V; and the Bow Trio, a bow-shaped bead with three holes. The Honeycomb is a hexagonal two-hole bead.

Preciosa makes a two-hole cab called a Candy bead (shaped like an M&M) and an arc-shaped bead called the bow, which is similar to the Arcos. Miyuki makes a two-hole Tila and half-Tila.

Other Beads

In addition there are: ZoliDuos with left- and right-hand versions; similarly shaped paisley beads; the Silky and MiniSilky; three-hole rounds and faceted beads; Cali beads, three-hole pointed ovals drilled through the flat side; two-hole chili beads shaped like chilis; Emma beads, three-hole triangular beads with the holes going through each of the points; Es-O beads, a kind of shortened SuperDuo; kite beads; tangos; tipp, a hexagonal pyramid, cups, and two-hole pyramid beads also called studs in 6mm and 12mm sizes.

Working with Two-Hole Beads

I've had so much fun working with these new beads! I believe they are here to stay. I do have my favorites, and for this book, I've stayed with the ones that work well in continuous stitches. You'll find mainly SuperDuos, bricks, rullas, tiles, AVAs, two- and three-hole bars and beams, and studs.

Some of the other two-hole beads have limited use for continuous stitches, but I see them in a lot of round and dimensional work, and they look great. Some two-hole beads don't match the thickness of other beads, and two-hole triangles are very difficult to get turned the right way. However, they look great incorporated in round and three-dimensional work.

But don't let my choices deter you from trying anything that comes into your head! In spite of the great number of options in this book, I've only scratched the surface of what can be done with these beads. I hope you'll join me in exploring and creating with them.

Challenges with Two-Hole Beads

Clogged Holes: One of the biggest worries when working with these beads is finding one of the holes plugged after you've incorporated it into the work. After this happened to me the first, second, and third times, I started testing the holes. This usually only happens with pressed glass beads and the narrower beads such as SuperDuos and twins, Rullas, and bricks. The condition is worse when there is a coating of some kind. I have not had problems with the larger beads like tiles and studs. You may want to just poke out the hole, but don't do it—you may create a very sharp break right where the thread rubs, and this can cut the thread. Just throw that bead away!

If you ever encounter a clogged hole and have to take apart a section of work, or worse—make it over, you will understand the need to test each hole. I simply poke my needle through one of the holes, and if it goes all the way through, I go into the other hole and use it to pick up the bead.

With SuperDuos, there is an even simpler way to deal with this. Get a bead bowl that is a contrasting color (mine are white). The SuperDuos will tilt when laying and you are in position to look through the upper hole and see that it's open. Then, you can just pick up the bead with the lower hole and know that both holes are open.

Broken Beads: I find that Tilas have sharper edges and like to break at the corners. Work looser than usual to prevent the Tilas from rubbing or pressing against one another when moving. You won't have this problem with pressed glass beads.

Size: Coating will add to the size of any bead. Sometimes manufacturers will make the beads slightly smaller to take up the difference, and sometimes they won't. When mixing colors or finishes in a piece, notice whether you have this type of size difference.

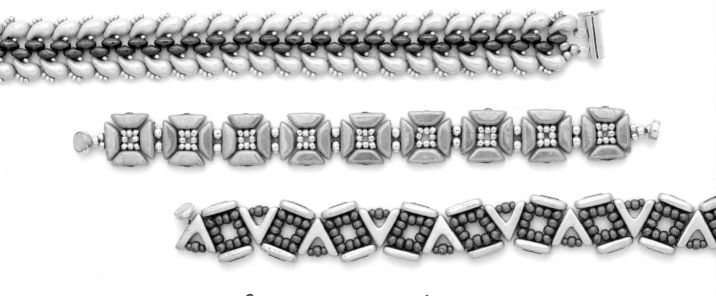

Now you're ready, so let's bead! Remember to relax, stop and stretch, or walk around every now and then. Most importantly: *have fun!*

Section 1
STRINGING

Sometimes easy pieces are just what we need: a quick gift for a friend, a special bracelet for a child, or a simple piece you can teach easily to someone else.

Stringing is simply a one-off set of instructions. There is no repeatable or well-defined stitch, but simply instructions to make one particular piece. Stringing need not be just adding one bead after another on a thread. Some pieces can be quite complex. While my own jewelry-making inclination is toward bead weaving because of the intricacies and patterns the stitches create, some of the most popular pieces I've made have been strung.

Wavin' Ava

BRACELET AND NECKLACE

Sometimes the simplest combinations can result in a striking effect. This is an easy project made using stringing techniques. I like the combination of silver or gold AVA beads and 6º seed beads in a contrasting color. Imagine this piece in gold with hunter green or gypsy red, for example.

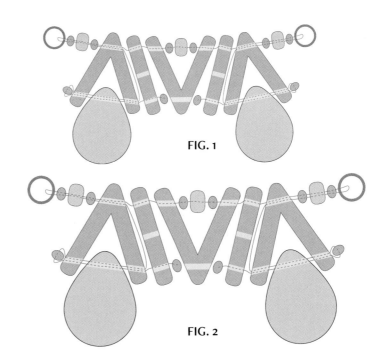

FIG. 1

FIG. 2

supplies

- **14** three-hole AVA beads
- **13** three-hole beam beads
- **16** 6º seed beads
- **26** 11º seed beads
- **1** toggle bracelet clasp
- **2** #10 or #11 beading needles
- 10 lb. test Power Pro or similar thread

Make the Bracelet

1 [**FIG. 1, red thread**] Cut 24 in. (61cm) of thread, and fold it in the center. Thread a needle on each end. Attach the folded center to one half of the clasp with a lark's head knot. With one needle, pick up an 11º seed bead, a 6º seed bead, an 11º, an AVA bead (the tip), * a beam bead (end hole), an AVA (a leg), an 11º, a 6º, and an 11º, and sew through the other leg of the same AVA. Pick up a beam (end hole) and a new AVA (the tip), and continue from *. With the other needle, pick up two 11ºs, ** and sew through the first AVA (one leg), pick up an 11º, 6º, and 11º, and sew through the existing AVA (other leg), beam (other end hole), AVA (tip), and beam (other end hole). Repeat from ** until you reach the desired length.

2 At the end, pick up two 11ºs with one needle and an 11º, 6º, and 11º with the other needle, and sew through the other half of the clasp and back through the beads just picked up to match the first end. Sew back through the beadwork, and end the threads.

Make a Necklace

To make this bracelet design curve into a necklace, add 11ºs on either side of the tip of the Ava along the bottom edge only [**FIG. 2**]. Fancy up the look with any large bead or drop that fits into the AVA along the bottom edge. I've used lovely 12x16mm pear-shaped drops from Czech.

Note: To make the necklace as shown, add a row of AVAs along the bottom edge. Simply pick up an AVA (narrow end), then add another row to add the 11º, 6º, and 11º, and attach the two round beads to the AVA above with seed beads.

Running River

NECKLACE

This radiating semi-collar goes together easily in one pass. It drapes nicely, as long as you maintain the tension and some weight to help the drops hang. Hang this partial collar from a strand of beads or a chain for a frontal statement.

1 [**FIG. 1, red thread**] Thread a needle on a comfortable length of thread, and tie a knot around a soldered jump ring. * Pick up a brick bead, an 11º seed bead, a brick, an 11º, an 8º seed bead, a drop bead, and an 11º. Sew back through the drop and 8º. Pick up an 11º, and sew up through the empty hole of the brick. Pick up an 11º, and sew through the empty hole of the next brick. Pick up a new brick and two 11ºs, turn, and sew through the other hole of the same brick. Repeat from * until you reach the desired length. The running stitch is a simple stringing process; tension is important. You don't want gaps between your beads, so be sure to take up any slack as you go.

2 [**FIG. 1, blue thread**] At the end, sew through another soldered jump ring, and make another pass through the upper two beads to strengthen the base. Sew through the beadwork, and end the threads. Finish the rest of the necklace off with your choice of chain or beads. (I like having an adjustable chain so I can wear the swag up high inside a shirt collar or down low over a high neck.)

supplies

- **83** two-hole brick beads
- **2g** 11º seed beads
- **1g** 8º seed beads
- **28** drop beads of your choice
- **2** soldered jump rings
- 18 in. (46cm) of matching beads for supporting strand and clasp
- #10 or #11 beading needle
- 10 lb. test Power Pro or similar thread

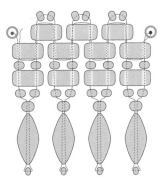

FIG. 1

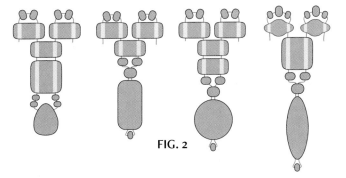

FIG. 2

Options

[**FIG. 2, red thread**] Many combinations can be made using different two-hole beads. Adorn the sections with large beads, drops, tubes, or spears for a fun necklace. Add a special focal piece at the center of the necklace to create a unique design.

Buds & Studs

BRACELET AND NECKLACE

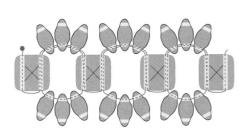

FIG. 1

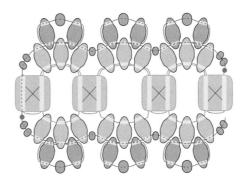

FIG. 2

A delicate color combination makes a lovely pattern with little flower buds seeming to extend along both sides. This design could also work in bright, flowery colors.

supplies

- **17** 8mm two-hole pyramid stud beads
- **150** SuperDuo beads (**90** color A, **60** color B)
- **1g** 8º seed beads
- **1g** 11º seed beads
- **1** toggle clasp
- #10 or #11 beading needle
- 10 lb. test Power Pro or similar thread

note

Make sure the studs are facing forward.

Make the Bracelet

1 **[FIG. 1, red thread]** Thread a needle on a comfortable length of thread. Pick up a pyramid stud bead, turn, and sew through the other hole of the same stud. Pick up three SuperDuo beads, a stud, and three SuperDuos. * Working in the same direction, sew through the first stud, the same holes of the SuperDuos, and the second stud. Turn and sew through the other hole of the second stud. Pick up three SuperDuos, a stud, and three SuperDuos. Repeat from * until you reach the desired length, ending by exiting a stud (second hole).

2 **[FIG. 2, red thread]** Pick up two 11º seed beads, and sew through the empty hole of the nearest SuperDuo. * Pick up a new SuperDuo, and sew through the empty hole of the second SuperDuo. Pick up another new SuperDuo, turn, and sew through the empty hole of the SuperDuo you are exiting in the other direction. Pull the SuperDuo up against the work. Pick up an 8º seed bead, and sew back through the empty hole of the other new SuperDuo. Turn again, and sew through the lower hole of the new SuperDuo you are exiting, the upper hole of the middle SuperDuo below, and the lower hole of the other new SuperDuo. Continue through the upper hole of the third SuperDuo. Pick up an 11º, and sew through the empty hole of the first SuperDuo of the next triple group. Repeat from * until you finish the side. Pick up two 11ºs, and cross to the other side of the bracelet. **[FIG. 2, blue thread]** Repeat on the other side.

3 To attach a clasp, exit a pair of 11ºs at one end, and pick up four 11ºs and half of the clasp. Sew back through all six 11ºs and into the beadwork. Repeat on the other side, sewing through the same clasp half. Repeat on the other end with the other clasp half. End the threads.

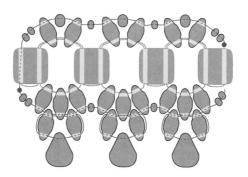

FIG. 3

additional supplies

- **17** 12mm drop beads
- 8º seed beads plus beads desired for stringing

note

Substitute tile beads for the pyramid stube beads in this necklace.

Create a Necklace

Making the bracelet curve into a necklace requires only a few small changes. This piece can be as long as you like—a full collar, or just a front section. As a necklace, the same technique takes on an Egyptian look. Go dramatic with deep red or black, or go elegant with black and silver.

1 **[FIG. 3, red thread]** Refer to the illustration to make a base similar to the bracelet, but on the top row, pick up only two SuperDuos. Make the bottom the same as the bracelet. Finish the top as shown, making sure you don't pull the thread so tight that it warps the piece.

2 **[FIG. 3, blue thread]** Make the bottom of the necklace in the same way you completed the bracelet, substituting drop beads for the 8ºs. Check the curve as you go, and add or subtract beads if the piece curves too sharply for your neck size. To finish, exit the top pair of 11ºs on one side, and string your desired pattern. Pick up half of the clasp, and sew back through the beadwork. End the threads.

Options

Use a square, Rullas, bricks, or even a box of cubes in the center instead of a tile bead. You can also replace the drop at the tip with a number of other beads, such as rounds, rizos, and even daggers for a more dramatic effect.

Dots & Dashes

NECKLACE

Elegant in any color, this narrow collar is easy to make. The dashes are 15mm two-hole bar beads, and the dots are 8º seed beads. The construction requires three passes with the thread. You can complete these passes with one long thread or work in three different sections. I prefer to attach a centered 2½-yd. (2.2m) thread to a jump ring and use one side for the first pass and the other side for the second pass, then attach a new thread for the third pass.

supplies

- **24** 15mm two-hole bar beads
- **240** SuperDuo beads
- **3g** 8º seed beads
- **.5g** 11º seed beads
- **1g** 15º seed beads
- **1** single-strand clasp
- **2** 4mm soldered jump rings (optional)
- **2** 4mm open jump rings (optional)
- **1** stop bead
- **2** #10 or #11 beading needles
- 10 lb. test Power Pro or similar thread

notes

- ◆ Be sure to use 15mm two-hole bar beads. CzechMates bar beads are too small for this design.
- ◆ On the bottom row, you can replace the 8º seed beads with tiny drops, and the 8º at the point with an even larger drop or a small dagger.

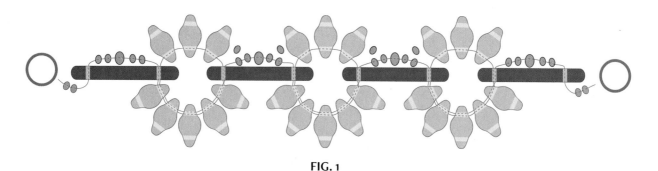

FIG. 1

Make the Necklace

1 **[FIG. 1, red thread]** Fold 2½ yd. (2.2m) of thread in half, and attach the loop to a soldered jump ring or clasp ring with a lark's head knot. Thread a needle on the bottom thread, and pick up two 15º seed beads, a bar bead (end hole), * two 15ºs, an 11º seed bead, and two 15ºs. Sew through the other end hole of the bar. Pick up five SuperDuo beads, a bar (end hole), and three SuperDuos. Sew through the last bar, all five SuperDuos, and the next bar. Repeat from * until you reach the desired length. Pick up two 15ºs, an 11º, and two 15ºs. Sew through the other end hole of the bar in the opposite direction. Pick up two 15ºs. Add a stop bead while you work the other thread.

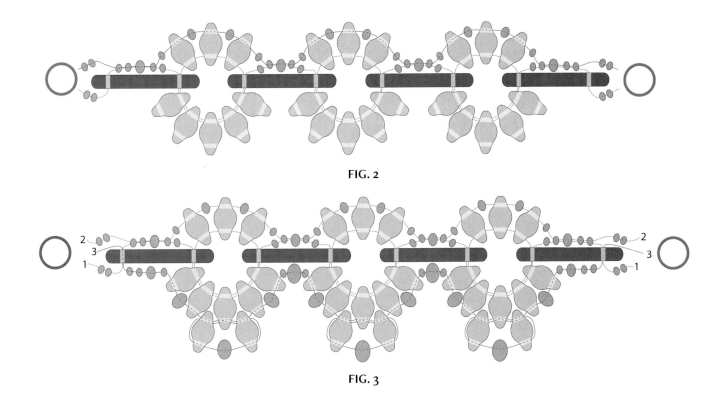

FIG. 2

FIG. 3

2 **[FIG. 2, red thread]** Thread a needle on the other thread attached to the original jump ring or clasp. Pick up two 15ºs, and sew through the two 15ºs, the 11º, and one 15º. * Pick up a 15º, and sew through the empty hole of the first (of three) SuperDuos. Pick up an 11º, and sew through the empty hole of the next SuperDuo. Repeat this stitch. Pick up a 15º, and sew through the second 15º and the next 11º and 15º. Repeat from * until you reach the final two 15ºs. Pick up two 15ºs, and use the two ends to attach a soldered jump ring or clasp. End the threads.

3 **[FIG. 3, red thread]** Place a stop bead 8 in. (20cm) from the tail of a new thread. Sew down through the first hole of the first bar. Pick up two 15ºs, an 11º, and a 15º. * Sew through the empty hole of the first of the five original SuperDuos. Pick up an 8º, and sew through the empty hole of the second (of five) SuperDuo. Pick up a new SuperDuo, sew through the empty hole of the third SuperDuo, and pick up another SuperDuo. Turn and sew through the empty hole of the last new SuperDuo you picked up in the opposite direction. Pick up an 8º, sew through the empty hole of the first new SuperDuo, turn, and sew through the upper hole of the same SuperDuo in the opposite direction, the bottom hole of the center (third original) SuperDuo, the top hole of the second new SuperDuo, and the bottom hole of the fourth original SuperDuo. Tighten gently as you go to maintain the shape of the group. Pick up an 8º, and sew through the bottom hole of the fifth original SuperDuo. Pick up a 15º, an 8º, and a 15º, and repeat from * until you have sewn through the last SuperDuo. Pick up a 15º, an 11º, and two 15ºs, and sew up through the end hole of the last bar. Use the end threads to attach a clasp, work your way back into the piece, and end all the threads.

ROCOCO

PENDANT

Rococo style is characterized by lightness, elegance, and the exuberant use of curving, natural forms. ZoliDuo beads lend themselves perfectly to this style (see p. 48 for more information about ZoliDuos). Hang this lovely pendant on a chain or add beads to go around the neck. It's also perfect for a young girl's wardrobe.

supplies

- **4** two-hole right ZoliDuo beads
- **4** two-hole left ZoliDuo beads
- **2** SuperDuo beads
- **1** two-hole dagger bead
- **8** 11º seed beads, plus desired beads for necklace length
- **8** 15º seed beads, plus desired beads for necklace length
- **1** O-bead, 11º seed bead, or spacer
- **1** clasp
- **2** #10 or #11 beading needles
- 10 lb. test Power Pro or similar thread

FIG. 1

FIG. 2

1 **[FIG. 1, red and blue threads]** Center 1 yd. (.9m) of thread (at least 2 yd./1.8m if you are going to add beads and create a necklace) in the top hole of a two-hole dagger, and thread a needle on both ends. With the right needle, pick up a left ZoliDuo bead (through the narrow inner hole). Turn and sew back through the other hole. Pick up an O-bead and a right ZoliDuo bead (inner wide hole). With the left needle, sew through the inner narrow hole of the right ZoliDuo you just added. Turn, and sew back through the other hole of the same ZoliDuo and the O-bead, and continue through the inner wide hole of the first ZoliDuo.

2 **[FIG. 2, blue thread]** With the right needle, pick up two right ZoliDuos (outer narrow hole), a SuperDuo, and a left ZoliDuo (inner narrow hole). Sew through the outer narrow hole of the first ZoliDuo, and continue through the upper hole of the dagger. Turn and sew through the other hole of the dagger.

3 **[FIG. 2, red thread]** With the left needle, pick up two left ZoliDuos (outer narrow hole), a SuperDuo, and a right ZoliDuo (inner narrow hole). Sew through the outer narrow hole of the second ZoliDuo you picked up, and continue through the upper hole of the dagger. Turn and sew through the other hole of the dagger.

Note: Be sure your group of SuperDuos is turned so the threads are exiting the upper holes of the two center beads. It's very easy to get your ZoliDuo beads facing the wrong way. I suggest laying them out in the approximate pattern on your work table so they are facing the right way when you pick them up.

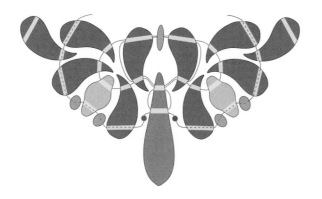

FIG. 3

FIG. 4

4 [FIG. 3, red thread] With the left needle, sew through the outer wide hole of the adjacent ZoliDuo. Pick up an 11º, and sew through the empty hole of the SuperDuo. Pick up an 11º, and sew through the inner wide hole of the next ZoliDuo. Pick up a right ZoliDuo by the outer narrow hole, and sew through the empty hole of the next ZoliDuo.

5 [FIG. 3, blue thread] With the right needle, sew through the outer wide hole of the adjacent ZoliDuo. Pick up an 11º, and sew through the empty hole of the Super-Duo. Pick up an 11º, and sew through the inner wide hole of the next ZoliDuo. Pick up a left ZoliDuo by the outer narrow hole, and sew through the empty hole of the next ZoliDuo.

6 [FIG. 4, red thread] With the left needle, pick up a 15º seed bead, an 11º, and a 15º. Sew through the outer narrow hole of the ZoliDuo you just exited. Continue through the inner hole of the next ZoliDuo, the SuperDuo, and the narrow holes of the next two ZoliDuos, and continue on through the upper hole of the dagger, the next two ZoliDuos, the other SuperDuo, and the next two ZoliDuos. Pick up a 15º, an 11º, and a 15º, and sew through the wide outer hole of the ZoliDuo you just exited. Continue through the narrow hole of the adjacent ZoliDuo. Pick up a 15º, an 11º, and a 15º, and sew through the empty hole of the same ZoliDuo.

7 [FIG. 4, blue thread] Mirror the path of the red thread. Pick up a 15º, an 11º, and a 15º. Sew through the outer narrow hole of the ZoliDuo you just exited. Continue through the narrow hole of the next ZoliDuo, the SuperDuo, and the narrow holes of the next two ZoliDuos, the upper hole of the dagger, the next two ZoliDuos, the other SuperDuo, and the next two ZoliDuos. Sew through the existing 15º, 11º, and 15º, and continue through the outer wide hole of the ZoliDuo you just exited and the narrow hole of the adjacent ZoliDuo. Pick up a 15º, an 11º, and a 15º. Turn, and sew through the empty hole of the same ZoliDuo.

8 Attach soldered jump rings to each side here for a chain, or string seed beads in a pattern of your choice to make a strand. Attach a clasp, and sew back through the beads and through the last two ZoliDuos, the 15º, 11º, and 15º, into the center grouping of ZoliDuo, spacer, and ZoliDuo. End the threads.

Section 2
EARRINGS

Sometimes earrings are overlooked in books of bracelets and necklaces. Even though the matchy-matchy look is out of style, I still may want accessories that go nicely with a project I've just made. In addition, I find I have a lot of leftover beads from these larger projects, and earrings are just the right size to use them up.

One consideration with earrings is not all people have pierced ears, while others are allergic to base metals. In consideration, I always make my earrings on a soldered jump ring. I keep these in my stock of findings in silver and gold. I use 22-gauge, 3mm or 4mm. That way, the earring back or ear wire can easily be changed to suit without undoing the beadwork. Plus, they hang straight and swing more freely than ear wires connected directly to loops of beads.

I like to create my earrings so there is a "face" to them. If the earrings are hung on a single line or a single bead, the earrings can rotate, turning front to back or side-ways. I usually attach the earrings at two points on the jump ring or I spread the thread apart with half-hitches so they face front.

A great pair of earrings should be allowed to show off, so don't distract from them with an elaborate neck-piece. A bracelet can be more suitable companion piece because it's further from the ears. On the other hand, if you're showing off a neckpiece, choose simple earrings.

Magic Circle

EARRINGS

The circle is magic because it can be made of so many different two-hole beads. Play around with the circle and the drop, depending on what beads you have available, to create many different looks.

supplies

- **2** 12x18mm drop beads
- **4** two-hole CzechMates tile beads
- **8** two-hole CzechMates brick beads
- **2** GemDuo diamonds or SuperDuo beads
- **1g** 11º seed beads
- **2** 4mm soldered jump rings
- **1** pair of ear wires
- **2** #10 or #11 beading needles
- **8** lb. test Power Pro or similar thread
- **2** pairs of chainnose pliers

1 **[FIG. 1, red thread, and FIG. 2, blue thread]** Thread a needle on each end of 2 ft. (61cm) of thread. With one needle, pick up three 11º seed beads, and center them on the thread. Pick up a brick bead, an 11º, a tile bead, an 11º, a brick, an 11º, and a GemDuo diamond. Repeat with the other needle on the other side, crossing through the same GemDuo. Check to see you are still centered on the thread, and with each needle, sew through the adjacent 11º and brick. Turn and sew back through the brick in the opposite direction. Pick up two 11ºs, and sew through the empty hole of the SuperDuo or GemDuo.

2 **[FIG. 1, red thread, and FIG. 2, blue thread]** You are ready to work the outside of the ring. Continue to work with both needles: Sew through the two 11ºs, and continue through the outside hole of the next brick. Pick up three 11ºs, and sew through the outside hole of the tile. Pick up three 11ºs, and sew through the outside hole of the brick. Pick up an 11º and a drop. Repeat on the other side, mirroring the action of the first thread. Cross the threads inside the drop, and snug up the beadwork. Continue with each needle around the outside all the way through to the two 11ºs at the top. Pick up two more 11ºs, and sew through the soldered jump ring. Turn and sew back through the two 11ºs you just picked up and the two 11ºs at the top of the ring. Continue through the beadwork, and end the threads. Attach an ear wire to the jump ring.

3 Repeat to make a second earring.

FIG. 1   FIG. 2

Options

- Replace the drop with a grouping of GemDuos.
- Use all bricks and enlarge the GemDuo group in the center.
- Replace the bricks with half-round beads; you will need to adjust the attachment of the drop.

27

Lady Harp

EARRINGS

I love the S-shaped Snake beads. Like the ZoliDuos, they lend themselves to fluid designs. Try to keep your work tight as you go. I like to take up slack every time the threads cross in the center; it keeps the piece from warping.

supplies

- **8** three-hole Snake trio beads
- **2** 7–8mm two-hole cabochons
- **6** 4mm round beads
- **2** 8º seed bead
- **12** 11º seed beads
- **4** 15º seed beads
- **2** 4mm soldered jump rings
- **1** pair of earring wires
- **2** #10 or #11 beading needles
- 8 lb. test Power Pro or similar thread
- **2** pairs of chainnose pliers

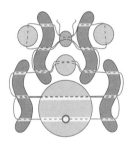

FIG. 1

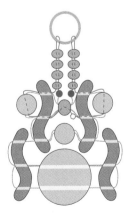

FIG. 2

1 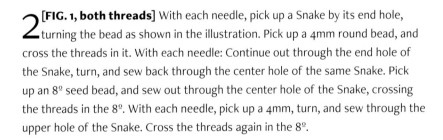 [**FIG. 1, both threads**] Thread a needle both ends of on 2 ft. (61cm) of thread. With one needle, pick up a two-hole cabochon through the left hole (when the holes are parallel, vertical, and the bead is facing up), and center it on the thread. Lay out the Snake beads as shown in the illustration. With one needle, pick up a Snake by the end hole. Turn and sew in the opposite direction through the center hole of the Snake, and continue through the other hole of the cabochon. Repeat with the other needle. With each needle, continue through the center hole of a Snake, turn, and sew through the other end hole of the Snake.

2 [**FIG. 1, both threads**] With each needle, pick up a Snake by its end hole, turning the bead as shown in the illustration. Pick up a 4mm round bead, and cross the threads in it. With each needle: Continue out through the end hole of the Snake, turn, and sew back through the center hole of the same Snake. Pick up an 8º seed bead, and sew out through the center hole of the Snake, crossing the threads in the 8º. With each needle, pick up a 4mm, turn, and sew through the upper hole of the Snake. Cross the threads again in the 8º.

3 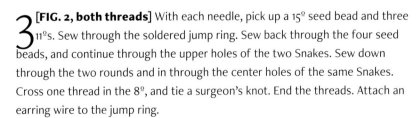 [**FIG. 2, both threads**] With each needle, pick up a 15º seed bead and three 11ºs. Sew through the soldered jump ring. Sew back through the four seed beads, and continue through the upper holes of the two Snakes. Sew down through the two rounds and in through the center holes of the same Snakes. Cross one thread in the 8º, and tie a surgeon's knot. End the threads. Attach an earring wire to the jump ring.

4 Make a second earring.

Dots & Dashes

EARRINGS

Match these up with the "Dots & Dashes Necklace," p. 19. These large, 15mm two-hole bar beads pair nicely with SuperDuos.

supplies

- **2** 15mm two-hole bar beads
- **20** SuperDuo beads
- **8** 8º seed beads
- **24** 11º seed beads
- **2** 4mm soldered jump rings
- **1** pair of earring wires
- **2** #10 or #11 beading needles
- 8 lb. test Power Pro or similar thread
- **2** pairs of chainnose pliers

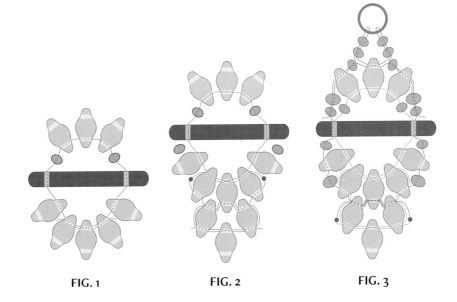

FIG. 1 **FIG. 2** **FIG. 3**

1 [**FIG. 1, red thread**] Thread a needle on each end of 2 ft. (61cm) of thread. With one needle, pick up four SuperDuo beads and a bar bead. Pick up an 11º seed bead, three SuperDuos, and an 11º, and sew through the other hole of the bar. Pick up a SuperDuo, and sew through the first three SuperDuos in the opposite direction. Snug up the beadwork.

2 [**FIG. 2, red thread**] Turn and sew through the other hole of the SuperDuo you are exiting. Pick up a SuperDuo, sew through the bottom hole of the center SuperDuo, and pick up another SuperDuo. Turn and sew through the bottom hole of the SuperDuo you are exiting. Pick up another SuperDuo, and sew out through the bottom hole of the opposite SuperDuo.

3 [**FIG. 2, blue thread**] With the other needle, mirror the action of the first needle, crossing the two threads through the last three SuperDuos.

4 [**FIG. 3, red thread**] With the other needle, turn and sew back through the three SuperDuos (top hole, bottom hole, and top hole). Continue through the next bottom hole of the next SuperDuo. Pick up an 8º seed bead, and sew through the bottom hole of the last SuperDuo. Pick up an 11º, and sew up through the right hole of the bar. Pick up an 11º and an 8º, and sew through the upper hole of the right upper SuperDuo. Pick up an 11º, and continue through the upper hole of the center SuperDuo. Pick up two 11ºs, and sew through the soldered jump ring. Turn and sew back through the two 11ºs, the 11º below, and the next SuperDuo.

5 [**FIG. 3, blue thread**] With the other needle, mirror the action of the first needle. End both threads. Make a second earring.

Option

For different looks, replace the bottom SuperDuo with a drop, dagger, or feature bead.

Snaky Curves

EARRINGS

My best designs come when I am working—not thinking or drawing. As I completed the previous design, I had only two Snake beads left. I challenged myself to use them some-how. Earlier, I had tried a SuperDuo in the inside curve of the Snake and decided to follow that lead. This is what happened.

supplies

- **2** three-hole Snake trio beads
- **2** 7–8mm two-hole cabochons
- **4** SuperDuo beads
- **2** 8º seed beads
- **8** 11º seed beads
- **18** 15º seed beads
- **2** 4mm soldered jump rings
- **1** pair of earring wires
- **2** #10 or #11 beading needles
- 8 lb. test Power Pro or similar thread
- **2** pairs of chainnose pliers

FIG. 1

1 **[FIG. 1, red thread]** Thread a needle on each end of 2 ft. (61cm) of thread. With one needle, pick up a two-hole cabochon, an 8º seed bead, and a 15º seed bead. Turn and sew through the 8º in the opposite direction, and continue through the empty hole of the cabochon. Center this grouping on the thread. With each needle, pick up a 15º, an 11º seed bead, and a 15º. With the right needle, pick up a SuperDuo bead and a Snake bead through the end hole, turned as shown in the illustration. With the other needle, sew through the same holes of the Snake and the SuperDuo in the opposite direction. (This is a good time to snug up your beadwork.)

2 With the left needle, turn and sew in through the center hole of the Snake. With the right needle, turn and sew in through the empty hole of the SuperDuo and the center hole of the Snake in the other direction, crossing the threads in the center hole of the Snake. With the needle exiting the left side of the Snake, pick up a SuperDuo. Turn and sew back through the other hole of the SuperDuo, and continue on through the upper hole of the Snake. With the needle exiting the right side of the Snake, turn and sew through the upper hole of the Snake and the upper hole of the SuperDuo.

3 With each needle, pick up a 15º, an 11º, and a 15º, and sew through the soldered jump ring. Turn and sew back through all three beads and into the upper holes of the Snake and SuperDuo. Work your way back down, and end the thread.

4 Make a second earring.

Option

After this piece was so successful, I decided to see if I could elongate it, and I love the look! Simply connect the two sections with seed beads.

Silky
Diamond
EARRINGS

These work best as two-toned earrings. Use contrast between the color of the beams and MiniSilky beads to make the design pop. For a different look, instead of adding a MiniSilky at the bottom, add a drop or feature bead.

supplies

- **8** three-hole beam beads
- **12** 5mm two-hole MiniSilky beads
- **8** 8º seed beads
- **28** 11º seed beads
- **8** 15º seed beads
- **2** 4mm soldered jump rings
- **1** pair of earring wires
- #10 or #11 beading needle
- 8 lb. test Power Pro or similar thread
- **2** pairs of chainnose pliers

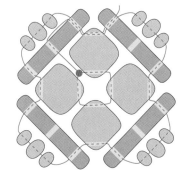

FIG. 1

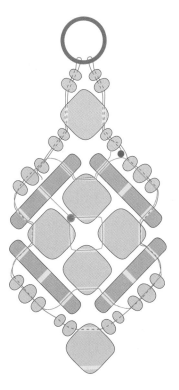

FIG. 2

1 **[FIG. 1, red thread]** Thread a needle on 2 ft. (61cm) of thread. Pick up four Mini-Silky beads, and pull them into a unit, being sure they all face up. Tie a knot to hold them tightly together, leaving a 6-in. (15cm) tail. Pick up a three-hole beam bead (center hole), and pull it flat against the nearest side of the diamond. Turn and sew back through the end hole to the right and through the outside corner hole of the adjacent MiniSilky. * Pick up a beam (end hole), an 11º seed bead, an 8º seed bead, and an 11º. Turn and sew in through the other end hole of the beam. Repeat twice from * until you arrive back at the first beam you picked up. Sew through the nearest end hole of the first beam. Pick up an 11º, an 8º, and an 11º, and sew through the far end hole of the beam, the MiniSilky, and the nearest end hole of the second beam.

2 **[FIG. 2, red thread]** Pick up an 11º and a 15º seed bead, a MiniSilky (right hole), an 11º, and a 15º, and sew through the jump ring.

Turn and sew back through all five beads you just picked up. Continue through the 11º, 8º, 11º, the end hole of the beam, the outside hole of the MiniSilky, and the end hole of the next beam. Sew through the 11º, an 8º, and the 11º. Pick up an 8º, an 11º, a MiniSilky (right hole), an 11º, and an 8º. Sew up to the other side through the 11º, 8º, 11º, beam, MiniSilky, beam, 11º, 8º, and 11º. Pick up an 11º and a 15º, sew through the empty left hole of the uppermost MiniSilky, pick up an 11º and a 15º, and sew through the jump ring. Turn and sew back through all five beads you just picked up, continue through the 11º, and turn into the work through the center hole of the beam. End the threads. Attach an earring wire to the jump ring.

3 Make a second earring.

Option
Adapt the ends to connect and string the units together to make a bracelet.

Zoli
Lotus
EARRINGS

These delicate earrings are reminiscent of summer nights on the River Nile. Make them in soft green or dangerous black with either silver or gold accents. You'll use curving ZoliDuos for this project (see p. 48 for more information about ZoliDuos.)

supplies

- **14** SuperDuo beads
- **6** two-hole right ZoliDuo beads
- **6** two-hole left ZoliDuo beads
- **8** 11º seed beads
- **16** 15º seed beads
- **1** pair of earring wires
- **2** 4mm soldered jump rings
- **2** #10 or #11 beading needles
- 8 lb. test Power Pro or similar thread
- **2** pairs of chainnose pliers

note

You can substitute larger 8º and 11º seed beads for the 11º and 15º seed beads.

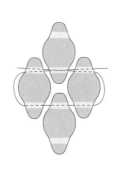

FIG. 1

FIG. 2

1 **[FIG. 1, red thread]** Thread a needle on each end of 1 yd. (.9m) of thread. With one needle, pick up three SuperDuo beads. Turn, and sew back through the other hole of the last SuperDuo in the opposite direction. Pick up a fourth SuperDuo, and sew through the remaining hole of the first SuperDuo. Center this group on the thread. With the other needle, repeat the first thread path in the opposite direction so the threads cross and exit opposite sides of the group. Be sure your group of SuperDuos is turned so the threads are exiting the upper holes of the two center beads.

2 **[FIG. 2, red thread]** With the first needle, pick up two right ZoliDuo beads (through the inner small end). Pick up a 15º seed bead, an 11º seed bead, and a 15º (or an 11º, 8º seed bead, and 11º; see materials note). Turn and sew in the opposite direction through the large end of the same right Zoli. Pick up a 15º, and sew through the large end of the ZoliDuo, going in the same direction. Pick up an 11º, and sew through the empty hole of the bottom SuperDuo.

3 **[FIG. 2, blue thread]** With the second needle, pick up two left ZoliDuo beads (inner small end). Pick up a 15º, an 11º, and a 15º, turn, and sew through the large end of the same left ZoliDuo in the opposite direction. Pick up a 15º, and sew through the large end hole of the next left ZoliDuo, going in the same direction. Pick up an 11º, and sew through the empty hole of the bottom SuperDuo. The two threads will cross here. Tighten.

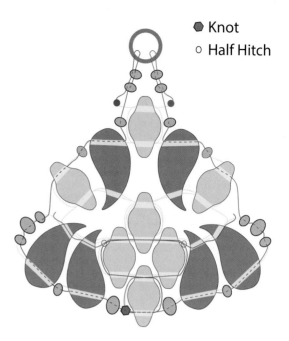

● Knot
○ Half Hitch

FIG. 3

FIG. 4

4 [FIG. 3, red thread] With the same needle, sew through the other hole of the SuperDuo above the one you're exiting, in the opposite direction, and continue on through the adjacent hole in the next SuperDuo. Turn and sew through the holes of all three SuperDuos above in the opposite direction, and continue through the two left ZoliDuos.

5 [FIG. 3, blue thread] With the second needle, repeat step 4.

6 [FIG. 3, red and blue threads, second dot] With the same needle, pick up a SuperDuo and a left ZoliDuo (inside small end), and continue through the empty hole of the top SuperDuo in the original cluster. Repeat with the other needle. The two threads should now be crossing inside the top SuperDuo. With both needles, sew through the ZoliDuos and the SuperDuos in the opposite direction again. Tighten.

7 [FIG. 3, red and blue threads, third dot] With the first needle, turn and sew through the upper hole of the SuperDuo in the opposite direction. Pick up a 15º, and

sew through the upper large end hole of the ZoliDuo. Repeat with the other needle in reverse. Pick up a new SuperDuo, and cross the threads in it. Pick up a 15º, turn, and cross the threads again through the upper hole of the same SuperDuo.

8 [FIG. 4, red and blue threads] With each needle, pick up two 15ºs and a soldered jump ring. Sew back through 15ºs and into the beadwork. End the threads (see below). Attach an earring wire to the jump ring.

9 Make a second earring.

End the Thread

In **FIG. 4**, I've shown you a path for ending the thread, since it is often hard to do so in such a small, delicate construction. After you attach the jump ring, follow the thread lines to the hexagon, tie a surgeon's knot, and pull the knot into the center SuperDuo. Then, follow the thread lines to the little ovals, and tie half-hitch knots to the crossing threads of the adjacent SuperDuos. Sew out through the ZoliDuo upper holes, and cut the thread.

Elegant Drop
EARRINGS

These earrings really do have an elegant look. They contrast the simple bold shape of the drop with the intricate interwoven shapes of the SuperDuos. Contrast against complexity is a characteristic of most interesting art.

supplies

- **2** 12x16mm pear-shaped drop beads
- **24** SuperDuo beads
- **8** 8º seed beads
- **18** 11º seed beads
- **2** 4mm soldered jump rings
- **1** pair of earring wires
- **2** #10 or #11 beading needles
- 8 lb. test Power Pro or similar thread
- **2** pairs of chainnose pliers

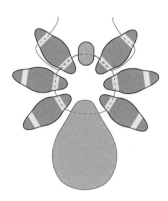

FIG. 1

1 **[FIG. 1, red and blue threads]** Cut 30 in. (76cm) of thread, and thread a needle on both ends. With one needle, pick up a SuperDuo bead, an 8º seed bead, three SuperDuos, a drop bead, and two SuperDuos. With the other needle, sew through the first SuperDuo, 8º, and SuperDuo. Center this group on the thread. Tighten. Sew both needles through the other holes of the SuperDuos you are exiting.

2 **[FIG. 2, red and blue threads]** With one needle, pick up a SuperDuo, an 11º seed bead, and a SuperDuo. With the other needle, sew through the same three holes in the opposite direction. Tighten. Sew both needles through the other holes of the SuperDuos you are exiting.

3 **[FIG. 2, red and blue threads]** With either needle, pick up two SuperDuos. With the other needle, sew through the same two holes in the opposite direction. Tighten. Sew both needles through the other holes of the SuperDuos you are exiting.

4 **[FIG. 2, red and blue threads]** With either needle, pick up an 8º and two 11ºs. Pick up a soldered jump ring, and sew back through the two 11ºs and the 8º, and continue through the top hole of the SuperDuo on the other side. With the other needle, sew through the existing 8º in the opposite direction. Pick up two 11ºs, sew through the jump ring again, and continue back through the 11º, 8º, and the SuperDuo on the other side. Tighten.

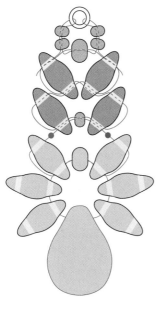

FIG. 2

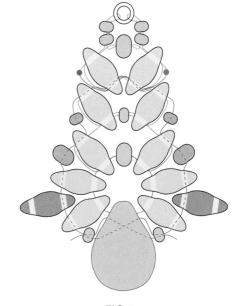

FIG. 3

5 **[FIG. 3, red and blue threads]** Sew through the bottom hole of the SuperDuo you are exiting. Continue through the lower hole of the adjacent SuperDuo and the upper hole of the next adjacent SuperDuo. Pick up an 11º, and sew down through the upper hole of the SuperDuo below. Pick up an 8º, and sew down through the upper hole of the next SuperDuo below. Pick up a SuperDuo, and sew out through the upper hole of the next lower SuperDuo. Pick up an 11º, and sew through the drop. Repeat with the other needle, and end the threads. Attach an earring wire to the soldered jump ring.

6 Make a second earring.

Tip: To keep your work really snug, every time you cross threads, pull equally on both threads to take up any slack. Also do this wherever the instructions say to tighten.

Egyptian Flare

EARRINGS

These earrings seem to lift themselves; they so want to fly. Perfect with a simple shift like the Ancient Egyptian women wore, this lightweight pair of earrings packs a lot of punch.

supplies

- **16** two-hole Tango beads
- **2** 4–6mm drop beads
- **44** 8º seed beads
- **12** 11º seed beads
- **2** 4mm soldered jump rings
- **1** pair of earring wires
- **2** #10 or #11 beading needles
- 8 lb. test Power Pro or similar thread

Note: A Tango bead is shaped like a right-angle triangle. It is reversible without any decorated face. You may have to rotate or turn it several times to get it the way you want it. In describing how to bead with these unique shapes, I developed a terminology to tell you where to insert the needle. There are two sides to enter: a flat side and an angled side. Also, the holes go through the narrow end or the wide end.

1 [FIG. 1, red and blue thread] Thread a needle on each end of 1 y. (.9m) of thread. Pick up a drop, and center it on the thread. With the right-hand needle, pick up an 11º seed bead, a Tango bead (from the narrow angled side), an 8º seed bead, and a Tango (narrow flat side). With the other needle, pick up an 11º, and sew through the Tango, 8º, and Tango again from the opposite direction. Turn, and sew through the wide angled hole of the Tango you are exiting, pick up an 8º, attach it to the 8º directly below, and continue through the other Tango (upper flat side). With the first needle, turn and sew through the upper hole of the Tango (wide angled side) again, the 8º, and the other Tango (wide flat side).

2 [FIG. 2, red thread] With the first needle, pick up an 8º, a Tango (narrow, angled side), three 8ºs, and a Tango (narrow, flat side).

3 [FIG. 2, blue thread] With the second needle, pick up an 8º, and sew through the narrow angled hole of the adjacent Tango and then through two of the 8ºs. Attach the last 8º to the 8º below it, pick up another 8º, and sew through the wide, flat hole of the adjacent Tango on the other side.

4 [FIG. 2, blue thread] With the first needle, turn and sew through the upper hole of the Tango you are exiting. Pick up three 8ºs, sew through the three 8ºs below, and sew back through the three 8ºs you just added in the same direction and the upper hole of the next Tango.

5 [FIG. 2, red thread] With the second needle, turn and sew through the upper hole of the Tango you are exiting. Sew through two of the 8ºs, attaching the second one to the one below. Sew through the remaining 8º, and continue through the upper hole of the Tango on the other side.

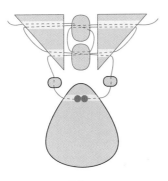

FIG. 1

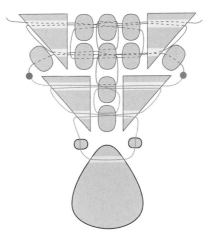

FIG. 2

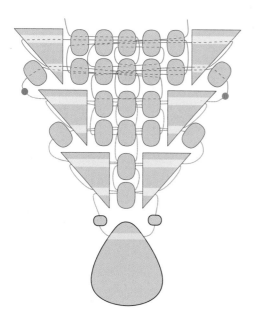

FIG. 3

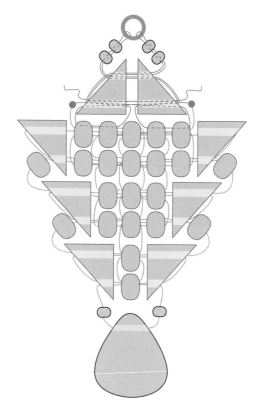

FIG. 4

6 **[FIG. 3, red thread]** With the first needle, pick up an 8º and a Tango (narrow, angled side). Pick up three 8ºs, and attach the last one to the center 8º below. Pick up two more 8ºs and a Tango (flat narrow side).

7 **[FIG. 3, blue thread]** With the second needle, pick up an 8º and sew through the last Tango picked up with the first needle (narrow, angled side). Sew through four of the 8ºs, and attach the last three of them to the three 8ºs below. Continue through the last 8º and the lower hole of the adjacent Tango.

8 **[FIG. 3, red and blue threads]** With the first needle, turn and sew through the upper hole of the Tango you are exiting. Pick up five 8ºs, and attach them to the five 8ºs below. With the second needle, turn and sew through the upper hole of the Tango you are exiting. Attach three of the 8ºs to three 8ºs below. Center each 8º over the 8º below. Then exit the row of 8ºs.

9 **[FIG. 4, red and blue thread]** With the first needle, pick up a Tango (wide, angled side) and attach it to the two 8ºs below. With the second needle, pick up a Tango (wide, angled side), and attach it to the two 8ºs below. With both needles, continue through the opposite Tangos (flat wide holes), crossing the threads. With both needles, turn and sew through the upper holes of both Tangos. Snug up the beadwork. With each needle, pick up two 11ºs and the soldered jump ring, and sew back through the 11ºs and into the beadwork. End the threads. Attach an earring wire to the jump ring.

10 Make a second earring.

Option
You can also use this design as a small pendant or charm.

Sweet Zolitude
EARRINGS

These earrings looks so simple, and yet it took me the better part of a day to determine the best thread path to hold them together well. I've inserted a point at which you tie a securing knot early on to keep the beads in place.

supplies

- **4** two-hole right ZoliDuo beads
- **4** two-hole left ZoliDuo beads
- **2** two-hole 8mm Candy beads
- **2** 12mm cabs or Candy beads
- **10** 11º seed beads
- **2** 4mm soldered jump rings
- **1** pair of earring wires
- **2** #10 or #11 beading needles
- 8 lb. test Power Pro or similar thread
- **2** pairs of chainnose pliers

It's very easy to get your ZoliDuo beads facing the wrong way. I suggest laying them out in the approximate pattern on your work table so they are there facing the right way when you pick them up.

1 [FIG. 1, red thread] Thread a needle on each end of 1 yd. (.9m) of thread. Pick up a left ZoliDuo bead by the inner wide hole. Turn, and sew back through the outer narrow hole. Pick up a cabochon by the right hole. Pick up a right ZoliDuo bead through the inner narrow hole, turn, and sew through the outer wide hole. Pick up an 11º seed bead. Center this grouping on the middle of the thread. Tie a surgeon's knot, and pull the knot into the 11º.

2 [FIG. 2, red thread] With the needle exiting the right side of the 11º, sew through the left hole of a Candy bead. Turn, and sew through the other hole in the opposite direction. Pick up a right ZoliDuo (inner narrow hole). Turn, and sew through the other hole. Continue through the upper hole of the left ZoliDuo below, and continue through the 11º. Turn and sew through the bottom (left) hole of the Candy bead in the opposite direction from the first pass. Turn again and sew through the other hole of the Candy bead.

3 [FIG. 3, blue thread] With the second needle, exit the left side of the original 11º and repeat step 2 in reverse.

● Knot

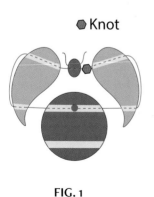

FIG. 1

FIG. 2

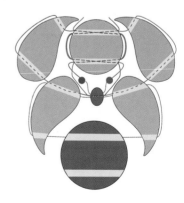

FIG. 3

4 [**FIG. 4, red and blue threads**] With each needle, pick up two 11ºs and the soldered jump ring, and sew back through the two 11ºs. With one needle, continue through the upper hole of the Candy bead. Tie a surgeon's knot, and pull the knot into the Candy bead. Work each needle through a few beads, and tie a half-hitch knot. Sew through a couple more beads, and cut the thread. Attach an earring wire to the jump ring.

5 Make a second earring.

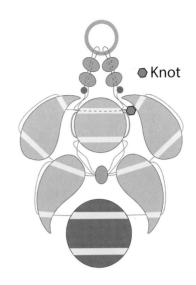

⬡ Knot

FIG. 4

Options

You can add 15º, 11º, and even 8º seed beads along the outside edges; you can substitute a larger bead like an 8º or 6º instead of the center 11º; you can add a drop or pyramid instead of the lower cab. You can replace the cab with a group of daggers, or anything else you can invent that fits.

Working with ZoliDuo Beads

◆ Which is right, and which is left? If you lay one of each ZoliDuo bead on a surface with the narrow (pointed) ends up and the outer (convex) sides out, they will look like parentheses: L is on the left, and R is on the right. There are two sides where you can go into a ZoliDuo: a convex side (outer) and a concave side (inner). The holes go through two ends: the narrow end and the wide end. For example, I will tell you to go into the inner narrow side and that will refer to only one hole.

◆ Right and left ZoliDuos can be confused easily. When working with them, I put the right beads in one bowl and the left in another. I place the bowls to the associated side of the work so that I go to the correct dish based on which side I'm working.

◆ ZoliDuos can be hard to pick up. You have both hands occupied, one holding the work and the other holding the needle. I use my little finger on my left hand without letting go of the work to put a bit of pressure on the other side of the ZoliDuo against the needle to help it through.

◆ If you are accustomed to turning the work after each row, you will not be able to do this easily because the ZoliDuos are one-faced. I keep the work in my left hand and let it grow out toward the right, adjusting slightly to adapt to the changing angle of the work.

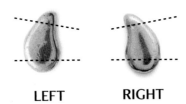

LEFT   RIGHT

Reverse Swirl

EARRINGS

This design is a swirling treat for the eye. You will have to make the second earring to mirror the first, not to be just like it. Simply lay out the ZoliDuo beads as you want them to go together using the alternate figures. It may seem that the ZoliDuos are right and left in each earring, but each earring is made with the same ZoliDuo—they only reverse position in the middle. (See p. 48 for more information about ZoliDuos.)

supplies

- **10** two-hole left ZoliDuo beads
- **10** two-hole right ZoliDuo beads
- **4** two-hole 8mm cabochons (or Candy beads)
- **24** 11º seed beads
- **24** 15º seed beads
- **2** 4mm soldered jump rings
- **1** pair of earring wires
- **2** #10 or #11 beading needles
- 8 lb. test Power Pro or similar thread
- stop bead
- **2** pairs of chainnose pliers

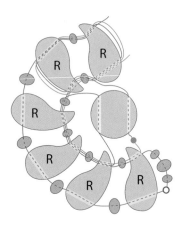

FIG. 1

1 **[FIG. 1, red thread]** Thread a needle on one end of 1 yd. (.9m) of thread. Pick up a right ZoliDuo bead (through the wide outer end) and an 11º seed bead four times, then pick up a right ZoliDuo (wide, outer end) and a 15º seed bead. Pick up a right ZoliDuo (inner, narrow end), and sew back through the free hole of that ZoliDuo, pick up a 15º, and sew back through the free hole of the adjacent ZoliDuo, the other hole of the same ZoliDuo, the last 15º, and the last ZoliDuo again. Center the beads on the thread. Attach a stop bead on the thread exiting the last ZoliDuo you added.

2 **[FIG. 1, blue thread]** Thread a needle on the other end of the thread. Pick up a 15º, an 11º, and a 15º, and sew through the empty hole of the same ZoliDuo. Pick up a 15º, and continue through the empty inner holes of the next three ZoliDuos, picking up a 15º after each. Pick up a two-hole cabochon (be certain it is facing front). Skip the first ZoliDuo, and sew through the next four ZoliDuos (and accompanying 15ºs) in the same direction. Sew through the next 15º and the empty hole of the cab. **[FIG. 1, green thread]** Continue through all the ZoliDuos and 15ºs again, plus the last right ZoliDuo (wide end). Reinforce the last four beads as in step 1.

3 **[FIG. 2, red thread]** Remove the stop bead, and thread a needle. Pick up a 15º and a right ZoliDuo (inner, narrow end). Repeat this stitch twice. Pick up a cab (facing up), and sew through the same three 15ºs and ZoliDuos again. Pick up a 15º, a right ZoliDuo, and a 15º, and sew through the empty hole of the cab and all five 15ºs and right ZoliDuos. Pick up a 15º, 11º, and 15º, turn, and sew through the empty hole of the last right ZoliDuo. Attach a stop bead.

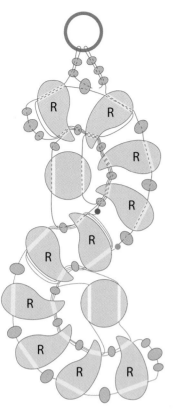

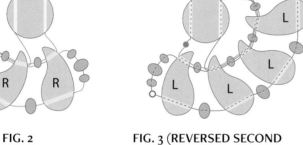

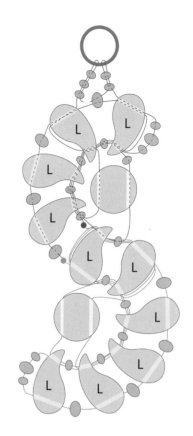

FIG. 2

FIG. 3 (REVERSED SECOND EARRING)

FIG. 4 (REVERSED SECOND EARRING)

4 **[FIG. 2, blue thread]** Pick up an 11º, and sew through the empty hole of the next ZoliDuo. Repeat this stitch three times to add an 11º between each ZoliDuo. Turn and sew back through the narrow outer hole of the last ZoliDuo, the 15º, and the adjacent ZoliDuo. Turn again and sew through the ZoliDuo you are exiting (wide end).

5 **[FIG. 2, red and blue threads]** Remove the stop beads. With the first needle, pick up two 15ºs and the soldered jump ring. Turn, and sew back through the two 15ºs. With the second needle, pick up three 15ºs, and sew through the jump ring and back through the three 15ºs. Cross both threads in the 11º below, and end the thread. Attach an earring wire to the jump ring.

6 Make the second earring the mirror image of the first (see **FIGS. 3 and 4** for the reversed version of the second earring). Substitute left ZoliDuo beads for right ZoliDuos in the instructions.

Option
Crisp white ZoliDuos with colorful cabochons and beads make a lovely, light summer look.

Fleur de Zoli

EARRINGS

This is my favorite earring design so far. It has a grace and beauty that shows off the best of the ZoliDuo shapes and blends perfectly with the cabochon beads. I love it in this aluminum color, which is soft with a gentle shine. (See p. 48 for more information about ZoliDuos.)

(See p. 48 for more information about ZoliDuos.)

supplies

- **10** two-hole left ZoliDuo beads
- **10** two-hole right ZoliDuo beads
- **6** two-hole cabochons
- **.5g** 15º seed beads
- **2** 8º seed beads
- **2** 4mm soldered jump rings
- **1** pair of earring wires
- **2** #10 or #11 beading needles
- 8 lb. test Power Pro or similar thread
- **2** pairs of chainnose pliers

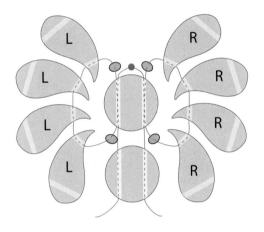

FIG. 1

1 [**FIG. 1, red and blue threads**] Thread a needle on each end of 1 yd. (.9m) of thread. With one needle, pick up a two-hole cabochon through both holes, and center it on the thread. With the left needle (thread path shown in red), pick up a 15º seed bead, four left ZoliDuo beads (through the inner narrow hole), and another 15º, and sew through the left side of the cab again in the same direction. Pick up another cab (left hole). Be sure the cabs are both facing up. With the other needle (thread path shown in blue) pick up a 15º, four right ZoliDuo beads (inner narrow hole), and a 15º, sew through the right side of the cab again in the same direction, and continue through the other hole of the new cab.

2 [**FIG. 2, red thread**] (Note: These threads overlap so much, it is difficult to illustrate. Work a short sequence with each needle, alternating between left and right.) With the left needle (thread path shown in red), sew through all the 15ºs and the inner wide holes of the left ZoliDuos. Pick up a right ZoliDuo and a 15º, turn, and sew back through the same hole of the ZoliDuo you were exiting. Continue through all the left ZoliDuos and 15ºs until you arrive back where you started. Pick up three 15ºs, an 8º seed bead, and three 15ºs, and sew up through all the 15ºs and inner wide holes of the right ZoliDuos on the other side. Pick up a left ZoliDuo and an 15º, turn, and sew back through the ZoliDuo. With the right needle [**FIG. 3, blue thread**], perform the same actions on the other side, mirroring the first side. At the bottom, sew through the 15ºs and 8ºs you picked up the first pass. Your threads will cross many times, but this will strengthen the connections.

3 [**FIG. 4, red and blue threads**] With the right needle, pick up three 15ºs, and sew through the empty hole of the adjacent ZoliDuo. Pick up a cab (left hole) and three 15ºs, turn, and sew through the other hole of the cab. With the left needle, pick up three 15ºs, and sew through the empty hole of the adjacent ZoliDuo. Continue through the lower hole of the cab in the opposite direction from the first pass, pick up three 15ºs on that side, turn again, and sew through the upper hole of the cab in the opposite direction from the first pass. With the right needle, pick up four 15ºs, sew through the soldered jump ring, turn, and sew back through all seven 15ºs below and the upper hole of the left ZoliDuo. With the left needle, pick up four 15ºs, and sew through the jump ring, turn, and sew back through all seven 15ºs below and the upper hole of the right ZoliDuo. Sew back into the beadwork, and end the threads.

4 Make a second earring.

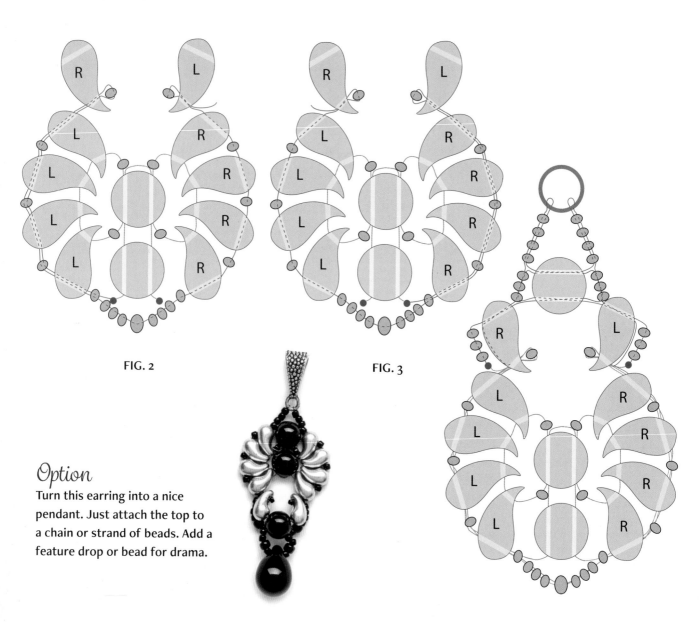

FIG. 2

FIG. 3

FIG. 4

Option

Turn this earring into a nice pendant. Just attach the top to a chain or strand of beads. Add a feature drop or bead for drama.

Section 3
S-BRAID

S-Braid is a stitch I introduced in my first book, *Stitching with Two-Hole Shaped Beads*. I love the simple, classic look of pieces done here using rullas and SuperDuos. With a few alterations, you can make the double-braid band curve into a beautiful necklace. By using graduated versions of the braid or a three-dimensional surface treatment, you can create a stunning feature necklace.

This is a versatile stitch that can be adapted to work with a great many sizes and shapes of two-hole beads. I was excited each time I tried it with a new bead, as it usually rewarded me with a great look. I've added ZoliDuos and QuadraTiles to the list of beads that work well in this stitch. I hope you'll explore some of the other possibilities as new two-hole beads become available.

You may recognize a few of these patterns from my previous two-hole book. It is necessary to have a foundation in this stitch in order to work some of the more difficult pieces, so I'm including them for anyone who needs an introduction.

As with many stitches, keeping the work taut is important. I pick up a sequence of beads, run the thread through, and wrap the thread around a finger of the hand holding the work. Then I make the next move, again locking the thread around a finger. I am right-handed and use the middle finger of my left hand as a "wrapping post" to keep the thread taut between actions.

Beautiful Braid

BRACELET

Requiring only seed beads and SuperDuos, this bracelet looks elegant in pearl and gold. Add a special gold clasp to finish the look.

supplies (white)

6-in. (15cm) bracelet, not including clasp

- **84** SuperDuo beads
- **124** 11º seed beads
- **124** 15º seed beads
- **1** toggle clasp
- #10 or #11 beading needle
- 10 lb. test Power Pro or similar thread

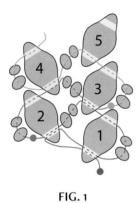

FIG. 1

1 **[FIG. 1, red thread]** Thread a needle on a comfortable length of thread. Pick up two SuperDuo beads, turn, and sew through the same hole of the first SuperDuo in the opposite direction. Butt the tip of the second bead against the hole of the first bead, and hold these two beads in place until you get a few more beads added. Pick up an 11º seed bead and a 15º seed bead, turn, and sew in through the empty hole of the first SuperDuo. Pick up a SuperDuo, a 15º, and an 11º, and sew out through the lower hole of the second SuperDuo. Turn the work.

2 **[FIG. 1, blue thread]** Begin the pattern: Pick up an 11º and a 15º, and sew in through the empty hole of the SuperDuo you just exited. Pick up a SuperDuo, a 15º, and an 11º, and sew through the first hole of the last SuperDuo on the other side.

3 **[FIG. 1, orange thread]** Turn and repeat step 2 until you reach the desired length.

4 This stitch creates an uneven end, so you will need to add 15ºs or 11ºs to fill the space needed to attach the clasp (see "Attaching clasps," p. 7). Remember to attach a row of beads to extend the bar portion of your toggle clasp so it will bend back and fit through the loop half. You can tell how many beads to add by making the extension just a bit longer than one arm of the bar. If your bracelet is very narrow, you may only need a short extension or none at all, as the bracelet itself may go through the loop. Attach the clasp and end the threads.

Option

You can use two 15ºs instead of an 11º and 15º. Experiment with other seed bead combinations that fit to further decorate the edge.

supplies (copper)

6¼ in. (15.9cm) bracelet, not including clasp

- **56** two-hole brick beads
- **28** 8º seed beads
- **112** 15º seed beads
- **1** toggle clasp
- #10 or #11 beading needle
- 10 lb. test Power Pro or similar thread

This copper version is a very pretty bracelet that holds together snugly with a shapely, braided look.

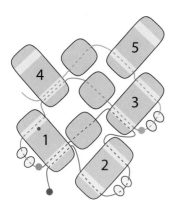

FIG. 2

1 **[FIG. 2, red thread]** Thread a needle on a comfortable length of thread. Pick up two brick beads and two 15º seed beads, turn, and sew up through the empty hole of the second brick. Pick up a brick and an 8º seed bead, and sew down through the lower hole of the first brick you picked up. Turn the work.

2 **[FIG. 2, blue thread]** Pick up two 15ºs, turn, and sew in through the empty hole of the first bead. Pick up a brick and an 8º, and sew down and out through the lower hole of the adjacent brick. Turn the work.

3 **[FIG. 2 , orange thread]** Begin the pattern: Pick up two 15ºs, turn, and sew through the open hole of the brick you just exited. Pick up a brick and an 8º, and sew down through the lower hole of the last brick on the other side. Turn the work. Repeat this step until you reach the desired length.

4 Add 8º seed beads or 15ºs to fill the space needed to attach the clasp (see "Attaching clasps," p. 7). Attach the clasp and end the thread.

Options

You can also use 4mm Czech cubes between the bricks. Their rounded corners and shape match the shape of the bricks. Use any bead that will fit, such as small faceted rounds, ovals, or glass or stone rounds.

Doubled Up
BRACELET

In this variation of S-braid, you'll increase the width by incorporating beads along the edge. S-braid amazes me with its flexibility. Essentially, you can make this bracelet with any number of two-hole beads. Try bricks, half-rounds, half-Tilas, or Storm-Duos. Once you get the hang of S-braid, you'll think of so many other two-hole beads to try.

supplies

6-in. (15cm) bracelet, not including clasp

- **50** Rulla beads (or brick beads)
- **50** SuperDuo beads
- **.5g** 15º seed beads
- **1** toggle clasp
- #10 or #11 beading needle
- 10 lb. test Power Pro or similar thread

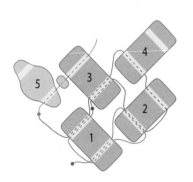

FIG. 1

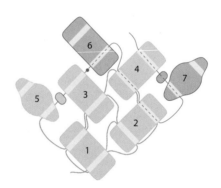

FIG. 2

1 [FIG. 1, red thread] Thread a needle on a comfortable length of thread. Pick up two Rulla beads (1 and 2), turn, and sew down through the same hole of the first Rulla in the opposite direction. Turn and sew up through the other hole of the first Rulla.

2 [FIG. 1, blue thread] Pick up a Rulla (3), and sew down through the lower hole of the adjacent Rulla (2). Turn and sew through the upper hole of the same Rulla. Pick up a Rulla (4), and sew down through the lower hole of the adjacent Rulla (3) and continue through the upper hole of the next Rulla (1).

3 [FIG. 1, orange thread] Pick up a SuperDuo bead and a 15º seed bead, and sew up through the upper hole of the adjacent Rulla (3).

4 **[FIG. 2, red thread]** Pick up a Rulla (6), turn, sew down through the lower hole of the adjacent Rulla (4), and continue down through the upper hole of the next Rulla (2). Pick up a SuperDuo and a 15º, and sew up through the upper hole of the adjacent Rulla (4).

5 **[FIG. 3, red thread]** Begin the pattern: Pick up a Rulla (8), and sew down through the two Rullas, the 15º, and the SuperDuo on the other side (lower, upper, then lower holes). Turn and sew in through the upper hole of the same SuperDuo. Pick up a 15º, a SuperDuo (9), and a 15º, and sew through the upper hole of the last Rulla on the side you are working (6). Turn and repeat this step, alternating sides, until you reach the desired length. Attach the clasp (see "Attaching clasps," p. 7), and end the threads.

FIG. 3

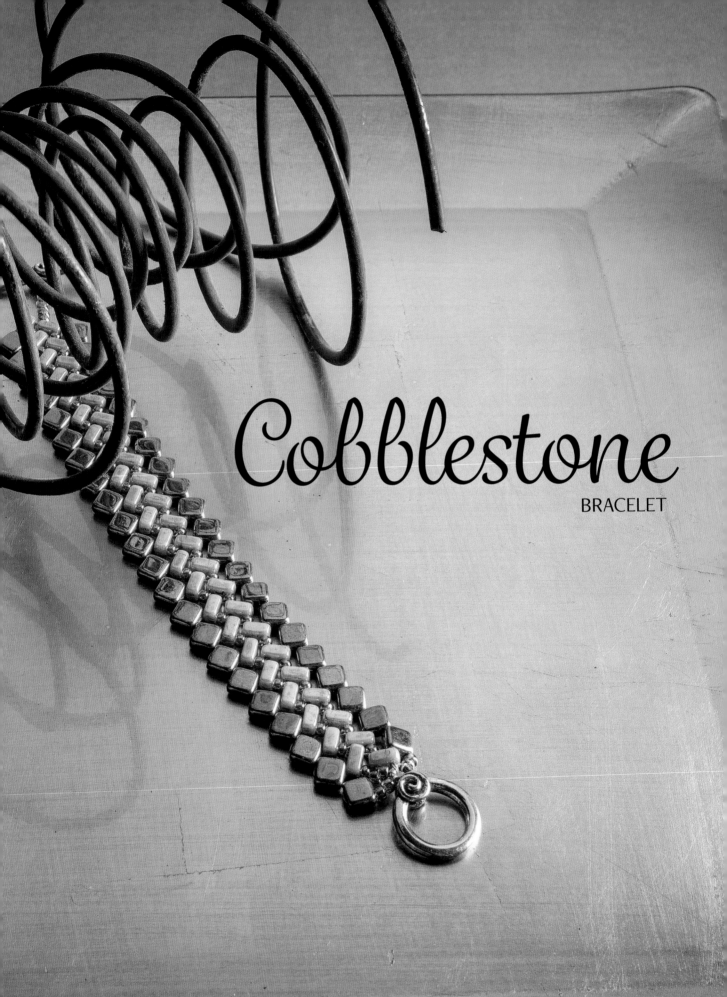

Cobblestone

BRACELET

supplies

6¼-in. (15.9cm) bracelet, not including clasp

- **50** two-hole brick beads
- **50** two-hole tile or Tila beads
- **2g** 8º seed beads
- **1** toggle clasp
- #10 or #11 beading needle
- 10 lb. test Power Pro or similar thread

This is a somewhat looser version of S-braid. The spacing between the larger beads leaves room for the eye to move through the design. Try other beads along the edge, such as hexagons or pyramids.

1 **[FIG. 1, red thread]** Thread a needle on 2 yd. (1.8m) of thread. Pick up a brick bead, an 8º seed bead, and a brick, and sew through the empty hole of the first brick in the opposite direction. Turn and sew through the first hole of the first brick again, and continue through the 8º.

2 **[FIG. 2, red thread]** Sew down through the lower hole of the second brick again. Turn, and sew up through the upper hole of the same brick. Pick up an 8º and a brick, and sew down through the previous 8º and brick. **[FIG. 2, blue thread]** Turn, pick up a tile bead, and sew up through the upper hole of the previous brick.

3 **[FIG. 3, red thread]** Pick up an 8º and a brick, and sew down through the previous 8º and the upper hole of the second brick.

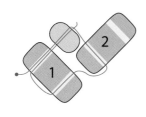

FIG. 1

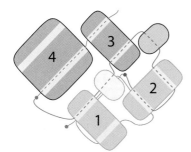

FIG. 2

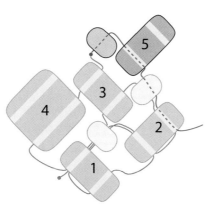

FIG. 3

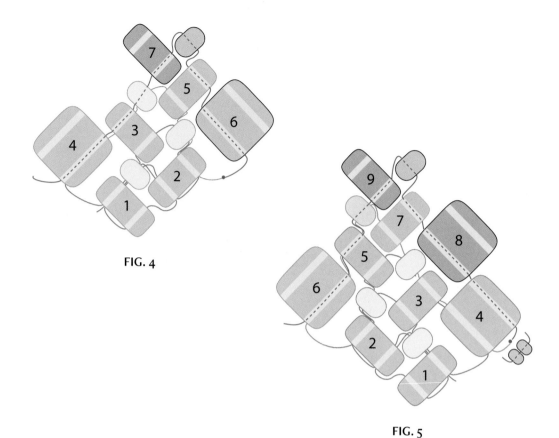

FIG. 4

FIG. 5

4 [**FIG. 4, red thread**] Pick up a tile, and sew up through the upper hole of the last brick. Pick up an 8º and a brick, turn, and sew down through the 8º. Continue through the upper hole of the left brick and lower hole of the left tile.

5 [**FIG. 5, red thread**] Begin the pattern: Turn the work left to right. Sew up through the upper hole of the right-most tile, pick up a tile, and continue up through the upper hole of the top-most brick. Pick up an 8º and a brick, turn, and sew down the left side through the 8º, the upper hole of the brick, and the lower hole of the tile. Repeat until you reach the desired length. Attach a clasp half at each end (see "Attaching clasps," p. 7). End the threads.

Options

Add a couple of seed beads to decorate the edge when you turn to go up the outside [**FIG. 5**]. To make a version with Tila beads, replace the tiles with Tilas and the bricks with half-Tilas. You can use any beads that fit into the spaces along the outer rows, such as a drop with spacing beads on either side, or a grouping that hangs down from the lower edge. One option is to double a narrower bead, such as a brick or Rulla, to replace one tile.

Graduated Braid
NECKLACE

I love the way this graduated neckpiece drapes around the neck. Because each side is made independently, you can add any number of focal bits at the center where the sides meet, and any number of edgings. I especially like the long line option, which often fits with tops when close neckpieces don't.

supplies

11-in. (28cm) main section, not including 8º seed bead extension, chain, or clasp

- **90** two-hole Rulla beads (or brick beads)
- **16** two-hole tile (or Tila) beads
- **5g** 8º seed beads, plus enough beads for the extension
- **1g** 11º seed beads
- **3** 10–12mm feature beads with one or two holes
- #10 or #11 beading needle
- 10 lb. test Power Pro or similar thread

Make each side separately, working back to front, and join them at the middle. Begin with 2 yd. (1.8m) of thread if you can, using a stop bead and a tail long enough to make the short section of strung beads and attach the clasp. You will want at least twice the length you anticipate plus enough to end the thread.

1 **[FIG. 1, red thread]** Thread a needle with 2 yd. (1.8m) of thread. The first section is the same as the "Beautiful Braid Bracelet" on p. 56. Make a few inches of this section. I made 9 rows (using 18 Rulla beads). You can further decorate the edge with a couple of 11º seed beads.

2 **[FIG. 2, red thread]** To transition to the next stage, stop with the beads placed as shown in **FIG. 1**. Pick up an 8º seed bead and a Rulla, and sew down through the lower hole of the last Rulla on the other side. Turn and sew up through the other hole of the same Rulla and the empty hole of the newest Rulla.

3 **[FIG. 2, blue thread]** Begin the pattern: Pick up an 8º and a Rulla. Sew down through the 8º and Rulla on the opposite side. Pick up two 8ºs, and sew in through through the upper hole of the Rulla you last picked up (4). Repeat until you are ready for the second transition. I made 5 rows (10 Rullas).

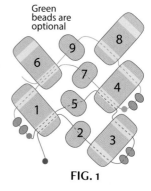

Green beads are optional

FIG. 1

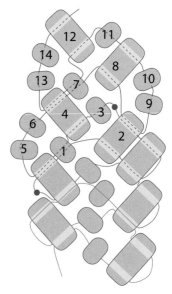

FIG. 2

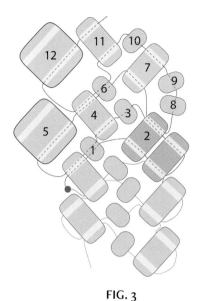

FIG. 3

4 **[FIG. 3, red thread]** Simply replace the two 8°s along the lower edge with a tile. Work until you reach the desired length. I made 8 rows (16 Rullas). This finishes one side. Repeat steps 1–4 to complete the other side.

Note: Notice where the doubled Rullas are (the green Rullas in FIG. 3). You will want the two sides to be mirror images, not to look alike, so when you begin adding the squares, be sure you are adding them to the lower edge in such a way that your sides mirror each other.

5 Join the two halves: You will want the last Rulla picked up to be on the bottom of each side of your work. From the top Rulla, attach one of the feature beads by sewing through it to the other side. Work into the piece to exit the bottom of the last square, and attach the other two feature beads. Mirror this action with the other thread. Use spacer beads, such as 11°s or 15°s, to ensure that the necklace hangs well around the neck. Repeat with the other thread to strengthen. Attach a clasp (see "Attaching clasps," p. 7).

Note: For the feature beads, two-hole pyramid hex or two-hole disk beads work well. This is also a great setting for a piece of bead embroidery.

Option 1
Replace the tiles (or alternate tiles) along the bottom edge with two daggers, or any kind of drop that will fit.

Option 2

For a very different long-line look, add squares along both sides. Attach them horizontally with two-hole beads in between and dangles.

Three-
Dimensional
COLLAR

supplies

14-in. (36cm) collar

- **106** two-hole tile beads
- **106** four-hole QuadraTile beads
- **212** 8° seed beads
- **212** 11° seed beads
- **106** 2mm round beads
- **53** alternate color 11° seed beads
- #10 or #11 beading needle
- 10 lb. test Power Pro or similar thread
- stop bead

note

This piece is closely related to the "Doubled Up Bracelet," p. 59.

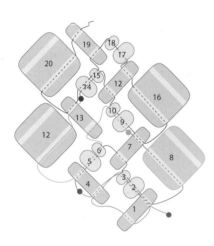

FIG. 1

If you have made the previous bracelets or necklaces, then you are well prepared for this gorgeous collar. Working with the QuadraTile beads is a challenge, but gaining the dimensionality is worth it. If going all the way around the neck seems a long way, then the half-collar is a great solution. Finish the sides with matching beads.

Using QuadraTiles means you have to be conscious of which hole you are going through. You want the two empty holes to stick up so that you can add the dimensional decoration onto the top of the work. If you miss the correct hole, the QuadraTiles can become angled halfway in and halfway out of the plane of the work.

One way is to work the piece in the hand, and I find it's best to have the side of the QuadraTile with the two empty holes extending down, that is sticking out under the work. Another way is to work flat on a surface and have the QuadraTile side with the empty holes sticking up. It may be easier to turn the work as you alternate sides, but this is a tactic you will have to work out yourself.

Make the Base

1 **[FIG. 1, red thread]** Thread a needle on a comfortable length of thread. Attach a stop bead, leaving at least a 10-in. (25cm) tail for attaching a clasp. Pick up a QuadraTile bead, an 8° seed bead, an 11° seed bead, and a QuadraTile, and sew through the remaining hole in the first QuadraTile in the opposite direction. Turn and sew through the first hole in the first QuadraTile again, and continue through the 8°, the 11°, and the second QuadraTile.

2 **[FIG. 1, blue thread]** Sew up through the remaining hole of the last Quadra-Tile, and pick up an 8°, an 11°, and a QuadraTile. Sew down through the 11°, 8°, and QuadraTile on the opposite side of the work. Pick up a tile bead, and sew up through the second hole of the last QuadraTile picked up.

3 **[FIG. 1, orange thread]** Begin the pattern: Pick up an 8°, an 11°, and a Quadra-Tile, and sew down through the 11°, 8°, and QuadraTile again on the opposite side of the work. Pick up a tile, and sew up through the second hole of the last QuadraTile you picked up.

4 **[FIG. 1, purple thread]** You have completed two passes of the pattern. Repeat steps 2–3 until you reach the desired length. Attach a clasp half on each end of the necklace (see "Attaching clasps," p. 7), and end the threads.

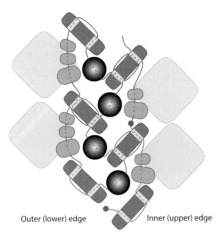

Outer (lower) edge   Inner (upper) edge

FIG. 2

Add the Raised Decoration

1 **[FIG. 2, red thread]** Attach a new thread and exit the QuadraTile nearest one end of the necklace. You will be working only in the empty upper two holes. Sew out through the hole nearest the center of the work. Turn, and sew in through the other hole.

2 **[FIG. 2, red thread]** Make an S-shaped motion with the thread. Along the upper (inner) side of the necklace, pick up an 8º and an 11º, and sew through the outside hole of the next QuadraTile on the upper side of the necklace. Turn and sew through the other hole of the same QuadraTile in the opposite direction. Pick up a 2mm round bead, and sew out through the inside hole of the QuadraTile slightly behind and on the other side of the work. Turn and sew in through the other hole of the same QuadraTile.

3 **[FIG. 2, red thread]** You are now working along the outer (lower) edge of the necklace. Pick up an 8º and two 11ºs, and sew through the outside hole of the next QuadraTile along the outer edge of the piece. Turn and sew though the other hole of the same QuadraTile in the opposite direction. Pick up a round bead, and sew through the inner hole of the previous QuadraTile on the other side. Turn and sew out through the other hole of the same QuadraTile. Repeat steps 2–3 **[FIG. 2, blue thread]** until you have finished the top decoration. End the threads.

Note: If you notice too much thread showing on either edge, adjust by adding 15ºs. 8ºs and 11ºs can vary quite a bit, and yours may not be exactly like mine.

Option

For this half-collar, I used bricks along the upper edge. This gives a sharper bend to the collar portion and helps the short curve hold its shape.

Symmetry
BRACELET

I was inspired by these mint green ZoliDuo beads to create a look mimicking the silver lace vine outside my studio window. The shapes capture the winding quality of these hardy vines. SuperDuo beads snug right into the arc of the ZoliDuos and keep your eye moving right along. (See p. 48 for more information about ZoliDuos.)

supplies

6⅞-in. (17.6cm) bracelet, not including clasp

- **25** two-hole left ZoliDuo beads
- **25** two-hole right ZoliDuo beads
- **50** SuperDuo beads
- **1g** 15º seed beads
- **1** 2-loop clasp
- **#10** or #11 beading needle
- 10 lb. test Power Pro or similar thread

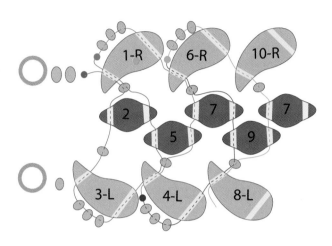

FIG. 1

1 **[FIG. 1, red thread]** Thread a needle with a comfortable length of thread. Pick up a right ZoliDuo bead (through the narrow outer hole), a 15º seed bead, a SuperDuo bead, a 15º, and a left ZoliDuo (narrow inside hole). Pull the beads snug. Pick up three 15ºs, and sew through the upper outside hole of the same ZoliDuo in the opposite direction. Pick up another left ZoliDuo, a 15º, and a SuperDuo, and sew through the remaining hole of the SuperDuo in the first row. Sew through the 15º below it and the narrow hole of the first right ZoliDuo.

Note: Here, you will have to squeeze your needle between the SuperDuo and the 15º. (It is easier to do this before you have pulled through from the previous beads, as the work is looser.) After you sew through the the 15º and ZoliDuo, pull the thread taut.

2 **[FIG. 1, blue thread]** Begin the pattern: Pick up three 15ºs, and sew through the upper outside hole of the same ZoliDuo in the opposite direction. Pick up a right ZoliDuo, a 15º, and a SuperDuo, and sew through the remaining hole of the SuperDuo in the previous row. Sew down through the 15º below and the lower hole of the next right ZoliDuo. Tighten the beadwork.

3 **[FIG. 1, purple thread thread]** Pick up three 15ºs, and sew through the upper outside hole of the same ZoliDuo in the opposite direction. Pick up a left ZoliDuo, a 15º, and a SuperDuo, sew through the remaining hole of the SuperDuo in the previous row, and continue down through the 15º below and the lower hole of the adjacent right ZoliDuo. Tighten the beadwork.

4 **[FIG. 1, orange thread thread]** Repeat steps 2–3 until you reach the desired length. Add beads to space out any difference between the bracelet and the clasp. Attach the clasp (see "Attaching clasps," p. 7), and end the threads.

Note: Turn the bracelet into a necklace by simply replacing the top row with SuperDuos and adding an 11º seed bead after each one [**FIG. 2**].

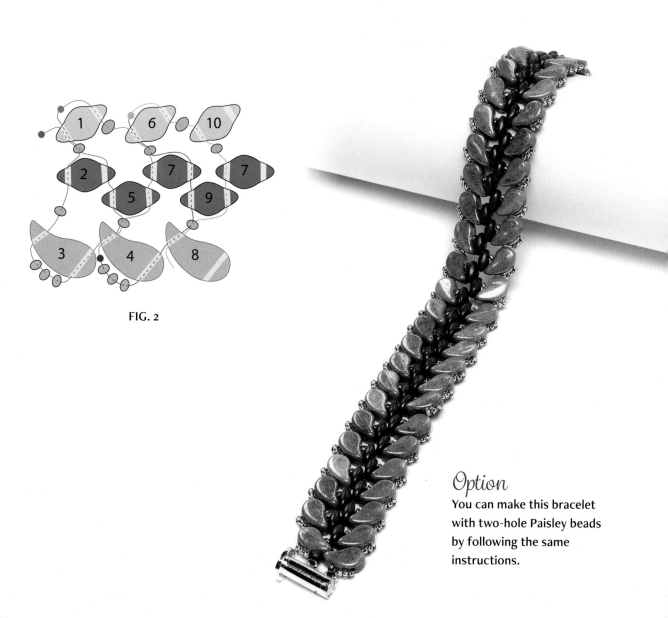

FIG. 2

Option

You can make this bracelet with two-hole Paisley beads by following the same instructions.

IRAW

IRAW (internal right-angle weave) is simply right-angle weave that is created inside a block of two-hole beads. Like RAW, it can go off in all directions to create double and triple rows, squares, diamonds, zig zags, and many other shapes.

I arranged my projects so the first ones are simple and provide a foundation for the more complex pieces to follow. If you find the later pieces to be too difficult, backtrack and make a simpler piece first. Once you get the hang of this stitch, it's great fun and very rewarding.

There are so many new two-hole beads available now that I have not been able to try them all. I love for my readers to apply their own creativity to these stitches. I hope some of you will try the two-hole beads that I have not, and do send me photos!

NOTE: Keeping the work taut is important. My process is to wrap the thread around a finger of the hand holding the work. I am right-handed and use the middle finger of my left hand as a "wrapping post" to keep the thread taut between actions and the fourth finger pressed against it to hold the thread in place. The action goes like this: pick up a sequence of beads, sew into the next series, release the wrap, pull the thread through and immediately make the wrap again without losing any tension. Repeat for each sequence, and you will have tight work.

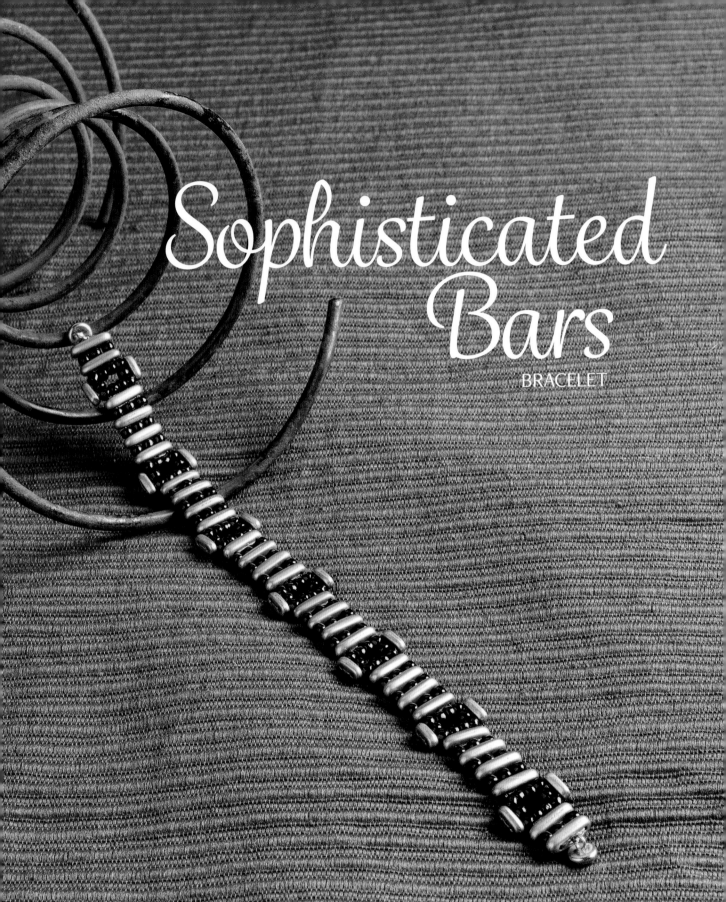

Sophisticated
Bars

BRACELET

Because IRAW is a bit complicated and at times takes solid management of the thread tension, I'm starting the section with an easy piece that uses large 8º seed beads. These beads are larger and easier to handle. If you are a skilled beader, go ahead with the smaller beads.

supplies

6⅝-in. (16.8cm) bracelet, not including clasp

- **28** three-hole beam beads
- **14** two-hole CzechMates bar beads
- **130** 8º seed beads
- **1** 1- or 2-ring clasp
- #10 or #11 beading needle
- 10 lb. test Power Pro or similar thread

1 **[FIG. 1, red thread]** Thread a needle on a comfortable length of thread. Leave a 12-in. (30cm) tail for attaching the clasp and the first two bars. Start with the IRAW square (later you can adjust the length by how many bars you add on either end). Pick up a beam bead (through an end hole), an 8º seed bead, and a bar bead, turn, and sew through the empty hole of the bar. Pick up an 8º and a beam (end hole), turn, and sew through the other end hole of the beam. Pick up an 8º and a bar, turn, and sew through the other hole of the bar. Pick up an 8º, and sew through the other end hole of the first beam you picked up.

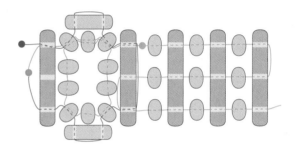

FIG. 1

2 **[FIG. 1, blue thread]** Sew through the first hole of the beam again, and continue through the adjacent 8º. Pick up an 8º, and sew through the next 8º around the inner beads. Pick up two 8ºs, and sew through the next 8º around the inner beads. Pick up an 8º, and sew through the next 8º around the inner beads. Pick up two 8ºs, sew through the three 8ºs at the top of the block, and continue through the top hole of the beam.

3 **[FIG. 1, orange thread]** Pick up an 8º, a beam (end hole), an 8º, a beam (end hole), an 8º, and a beam (end hole), turn, and sew back through the center hole of the same beam. Pick up an 8º, and sew through the center hole of the next beam. Pick up an 8º, and sew through the center hole of the next beam. Pick up an 8º, and sew through the center hole of the nearest beam in the block you just made. Turn and sew out through the bottom hole of that beam. Pick up an 8º, and sew through the last hole of the beams. Repeat this stitch twice. You now have a section. (Notice that if you turn the work upside down, your thread is exiting where you started, so you can make another IRAW block.) Repeat this entire block—steps 1–3—until you reach the desired length. If you wish to balance the design, you may go back to the beginning and add a section of beams and 8ºs. Add the clasp (see "Attaching clasps," p. 7), and end the threads.

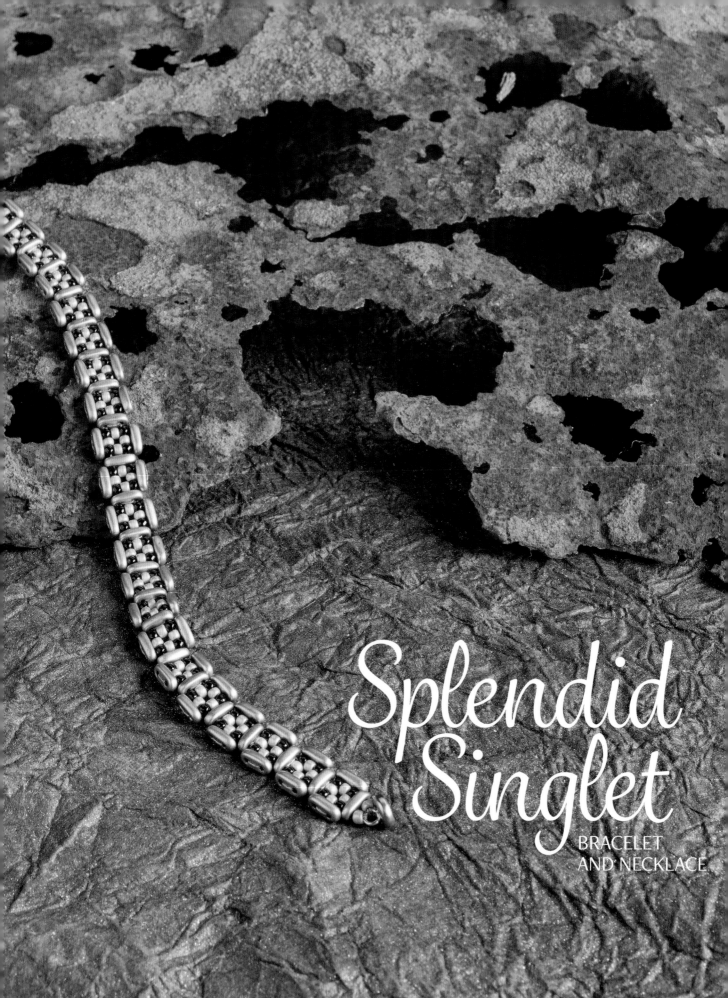

Splendid Singlet
BRACELET AND NECKLACE

Dainty and textured, this bracelet is simple but eye-catching. The contrast in the center section of the IRAW block keeps the eye entertained. Once you get the hang of the IRAW technique, I think you will find it exciting and want to incorporate other two-hole beads.

supplies

6⅝-in. (16.8cm) bracelet, not including clasp

- **67** two-hole bar beads
- **2g** 11° seed beads (**1g** color A, **1g** color B)
- **1** magnetic clasp
- #10 or #11 beading needle
- 10 lb. test Power Pro or similar thread

Make the Bracelet

1 **[FIG. 1, red thread]** Thread a needle with a comfortable length of thread. Pick up a bar bead, a color A 11° seed bead, and a bar, turn, and sew through the other hole of the bar. Pick up an A and a bar, turn, and sew through the other hole of the bar. Repeat this stitch. Pick up an A, and sew in through the empty hole of the first bar in the opposite direction.

2 **[FIG. 2, red thread]** Sew into the other hole of the first bar again, and continue on through the A. Pick up a color B 11°, and sew through the A at the next inside corner. Repeat this stitch three times to complete the round. Sew through the first new B and continue through the A and the adjacent hole of the third bar you picked up. This makes one block.

3 **[FIG. 3, gray thread]** You are in position to make the next block. Continue adding blocks of IRAW until you reach the desired length, and attach the clasp (see "Attaching clasps," p. 7). End the threads.

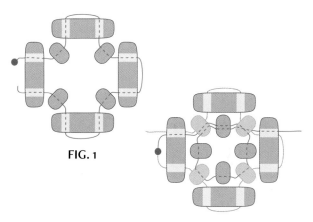

FIG. 1

FIG. 2

Options

Try this simple bracelet with a number of other two-hole beads, such as brick beads, or even three-hole Cali beads. Change the color pattern inside the blocks; add spacers as in the first bracelet.

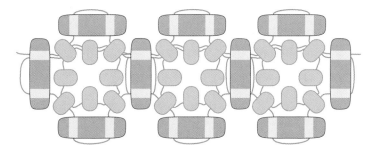

FIG. 3

supplies

18-in. (46cm) necklace, not including clasp

- **50+** two-hole brick and bar beads
- **2g+** 11º and 8º seed beads
- **24+** two-hole tile or stud beads
- beads for the strands on either side of the focal section
- **1** magnetic clasp
- #10 or #11 beading needle
- 10 lb. test Power Pro or similar thread

Make this necklace the same way you made the bracelet, except add a heavier bead along the bottom edge and extend it around the neck. The materials can vary, depending on the design. You can make a necklace that goes all the way around like a collar, or you can stop at any point and add beads on each side to finish off the length.

Make the Necklace

1 I like to start in the middle so I can see how long the center section will be and where I want to start to transition to the strands. I just take about 3 yd. (2.7m) of thread and center the thread on the first square, working out toward the sides.

2 Make the piece just as you would the simple bracelet, but using a square or stud on the lower side, a smaller bar bead on the top of the IRAW square, and an 8º seed bead in the bottom center of the square to allow for a slight curve. You can also add seed beads along the bottom edge as you go around the square or stud, or along the upper edge as well, if you like.

Options

Attach a pendant of bead embroidery to the center squares. Add anything that fits along the edge, such as feature beads or drops. You can even make a second pass and fancy up the edge with daggers and such. Play with the size and shape of the blocks of IRAW so to create variations.

Edging

There are different types of edging you can apply to bracelets and necklaces. If you use these on a necklace, be sure you are allowing for the bend, as some of these will actually tighten a side, and you don't want that on the lower edge where it needs to expand and curve.

Delicate

LARIAT

A fun piece to hang long or wrap a few times around your neck, this lariat shines in subtle colors. However, this piece lends itself to brilliant contrast as well. It will enhance the pattern in the 8º seed beads and make the centers of the IRAW blocks pop with color.

supplies

44-in. (1.12m) lariat with 31 blocks

- **124** two-hole bar beads
- **8g** 11º seed beads (**4g** color A, **4g** color B)
- **7g** 8º seed beads
- **2** 4mm closed jump rings
- **1** two-part clasp
- **2** #10 or #11 beading needles
- 10 lb. test Power Pro or similar thread
- stop bead

1 [FIG. 1, red and blue thread] Fold 3½ yd. (3.2m) of thread in half, and attach the fold to a clasp half (or soldered jump ring) using a lark's head knot. Thread a needle on both ends. On one needle, begin with a short strung section: Pick up an 8º seed bead, an 11º seed bead (alternate 11º colors as desired in the strung section), an 8º, a bar bead, five 11ºs, four 8ºs, and five 11ºs. With the other needle, sew through the first 8º. Pick up an 11º and an 8º, and sew through the other hole of the bar. Pick up five 11ºs and three 8ºs, attach the last two 8ºs to the center two 8ºs on the other strand, and continue, picking up an 8º and five 11ºs. Put a stop bead on the first thread. Use the second needle to make an IRAW block using bars and color A 11ºs. (See "Splendid Singlet," steps 1–3, p. 78.) When you have finished the block, remove the stop bead and bring the second needle through the bar, the three 11ºs, and a bar on the other side of the block. The needles should be exiting the two holes of the last bar.

2 Repeat the strung section and block to the desired length, alternating which thread you use to make the block and the strung section, so you have equal thread left on both sides. After the last block, add a strung section, and pick up a bar with each thread. With one needle, pick up an 8º, an 11º, an 8º, and the other half of the clasp. Sew back through the beads just picked up. With the other needle, pick up an 8º and an 11º, sew through the last 8º and clasp half, and go back through the beads into the beadwork. End the threads.

Note: If you are not going to wrap this necklace, you can make it without a clasp. Just begin with an IRAW block and end with the same block.

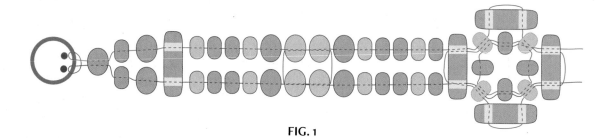

FIG. 1

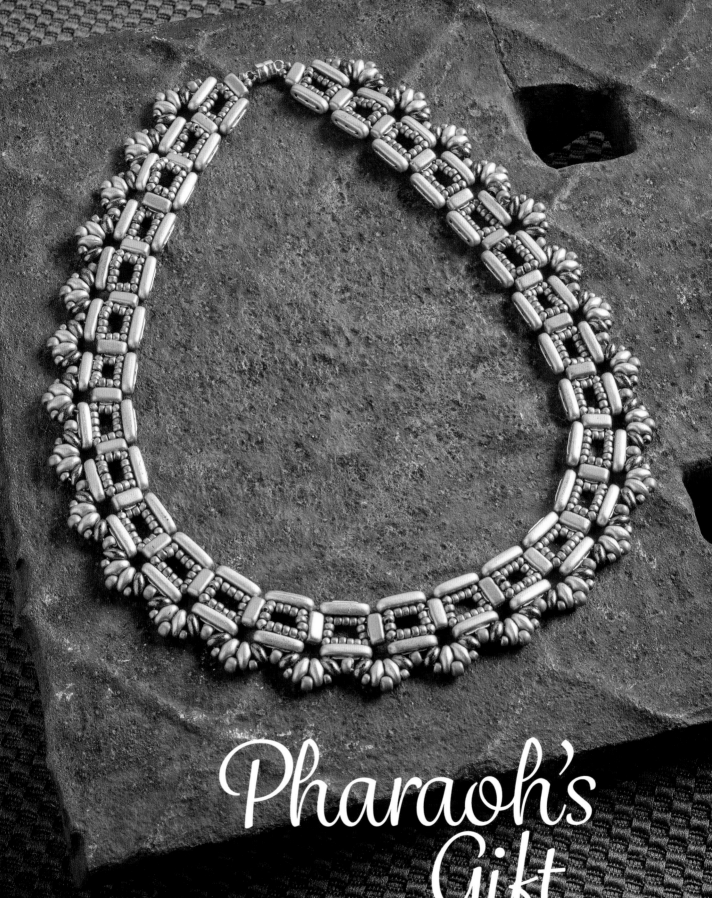

Pharaoh's Gift

NECKLACE

This piece is elegant enough to grace the neck of the queen. My favorite combination is the gold of Egypt with a gem color like lapis, carnelian, or turquoise. But I would also love a silver and black or copper and emerald color scheme.

supplies

16-in. (41cm) collar

- **60** three-hole beam beads
- **30** two-hole brick beads
- **112** SuperDuo beads (**56** color A, **56** color B)
- **4g** 11º seed beads
- **2g** 8º seed beads
- **1** magnetic clasp
- #10 or #11 beading needle
- 10 lb. test Power Pro or similar thread

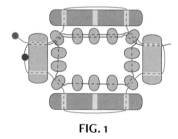

FIG. 1

1 **[FIG. 1, red thread]** Thread a needle on a comfortable length of thread. Pick up a brick bead, an 11º seed bead, and a beam bead (through an end hole), turn, and sew through the other end hole of the same beam. Pick up an 11º and a brick, turn, and sew through the other hole of the brick. Pick up an 11º and a beam (end hole), turn, and sew through the other end hole of the same beam. Pick up an 11º, and sew through the empty hole of the first brick.

2 **[FIG. 1, blue thread]** Turn and sew into the other hole of the brick again, and continue through the very first 11º. Pick up three 11ºs, and sew through the 11º in the next corner of the block. Pick up two 11ºs, and sew through the next corner 11º. Pick up three 11ºs, and sew through the next corner 11º. Pick up two 11ºs, and sew through the next corner 11º (the initial one). Continue through the next five 11ºs, and exit the upper hole of the brick. Continue building blocks until you reach the desired length.

3 **[FIG. 2, red thread]** Make the edging: Start or continue a thread from the end of the piece. Going up through the end hole of the first bottom beam, turn and sew down through the center hole of the same beam. Pick up an 8º seed bead, turn, and sew up through the same hole in the beam. Turn again, and sew down through the last hole of the same beam. Pick up four SuperDuos, and sew up through the nearest hole of the next beam. Turn and sew down through the center hole of the same beam. Repeat until you have finished the entire length of the necklace.

Option

Add decorative beads along the top
edge and replace the SuperDuos
with StormDuos, and the 8°s with
two-hole cabochons. Have fun with
other edging options.

4 [**FIG. 2, blue thread**] Make a second pass to finish off the edging: Sew down through
the end hole of the first bottom beam. Pick up an 11°, and sew through the first 8° and
the empty hole of the first SuperDuo. Pick up an 11°, and sew through the empty hole of the
second SuperDuo. Pick up an 8° (or feature bead), and sew through the empty hole of the
third SuperDuo. Pick up an 11°, and sew through the empty hole of the fourth SuperDuo and
the 8° you attached on the first pass. Repeat until you have finished the entire length. Attach
the clasp (see "Attaching clasps," p. 7), and end the threads.

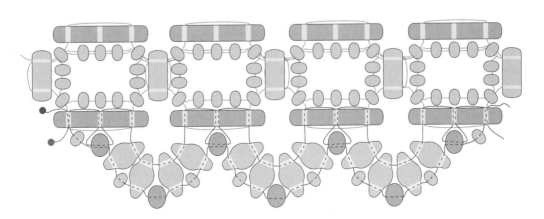

FIG. 2

Pharaoh's
Gift
BRACELET

This bracelet gives the beader a lot of options for color choices and patterns. If you need to change the length, there are two blocks for every edging section, so you may end up as I have with an extra block. Just fill in along the edge with seed beads.

supplies

7-in. (18cm) bracelet

- **34** three-hole beam beads
- **18** SuperDuo beads (or bars)
- **170** SuperDuos for edging
- **2g** 8º seed beads
- **3g** 11º seed beads
- **1** 2-loop clasp
- #10 or #11 beading needle
- 10 lb. test Power Pro or similar thread

1 Thread a needle on a comfortable length of thread. Leaving a 10-in. (25cm) tail to attach the clasp, follow steps 1–3 of "Pharoah's Gift Necklace," p. 83, and build a base to your desired length. Use SuperDuo beads instead of bar beads. When you finish the base, you can attach a clasp (see "Attaching clasps," p. 7), and end the threads.

2 [FIG. 1, red thread] Starting from the center hole of the first bar, pick up five SuperDuo beads, and sew up through the center hole of the next beam. Turn and sew down through the next end hole of the same beam. Pick up an 11º seed bead, an 8º seed bead, and an 11º, and sew up through the end hole of the next beam. Turn, and sew down through the center hole of the same beam. Repeat until you have finished the length of the bracelet.

3 [FIG. 1, blue thread] Exit the end hole of the first beam. Pick up an 11º, and sew through the empty hole of the first SuperDuo. Pick up an 11º, and sew through the empty hole of the second SuperDuo. Pick up an 8º, and sew through the empty hole of the third SuperDuo. Repeat for the fourth SuperDuo. Pick up an 11º, and sew through the empty hole of the last SuperDuo. Pick up an 11º, and sew through the 11º, 8º, and 11º you attached earlier. Repeat across the length of the bracelet. Repeat on the other side. End the threads.

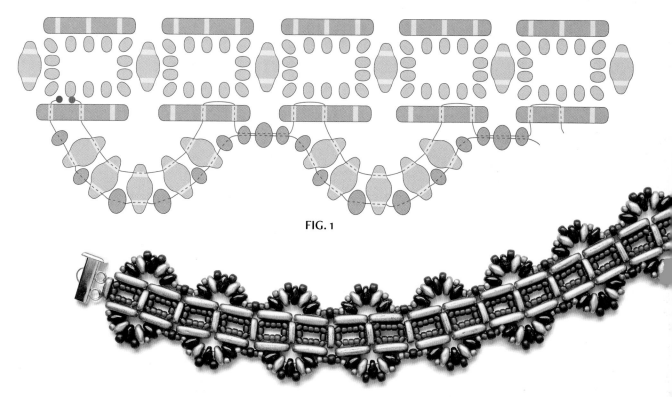

FIG. 1

Avas on Parade

BRACELET

IRAW is so versatile you can incorporate a number of different two- and three-hole beads into new designs. I've noticed that the shape of the AVAs are a bit inconsistent. Occasionally, you will find one shaped so differently from the others that the group of 11º, 8º, and 11º will not fit. Count on a few discards.

supplies

7-in. (18cm) bracelet

- **24** three-hole beam beads
- **10** three-hole AVA beads
- **4g** 8º seed beads
- **24** 11º seed beads
- **1** magnetic clasp
- #10 or #11 beading needle
- 10 lb. test Power Pro or similar thread

1 [FIG. 1, red thread] Thread a needle on a comfortable length of thread. Pick up a beam bead (through an end hole), an 8º seed bead, and a beam (end hole), turn, and sew through the other end hole of the last beam. Pick up an 8º and an AVA (through the outer side of the top of the V). Pick up an 11º seed bead, an 8º, and an 11º, and continue through the other side of the V. Turn and sew through the bottom hole of the same AVA. Pick up an 8º and a beam (end hole), turn, and sew through the other end hole of the same beam. Pick up an 8º, and sew through the empty end hole of the original beam.

Note: **Passing the needle through an AVA bead's top two holes is a bit awkward. You may have to go through one hole and pull through, pick up the three beads, and then go through the other hole of the AVA. Once tightened, the beads will snug into place.**

2 [FIG. 1, blue thread] Sew in through the original hole of the first beam, and continue through the first 8º. Pick up two 8ºs, and sew through the next 8º around the inner circle. Repeat three times. The last time, continue through the two new 8ºs, the old 8º, the AVA, and three-bead groups. You are at a position to repeat the section, only you will have the AVA in an upside-down position in relation to the first one. This will create a wave effect in the bracelet. Continue until you reach the desired length. Attach the clasp (see "Attaching clasps," p. 7). End the threads.

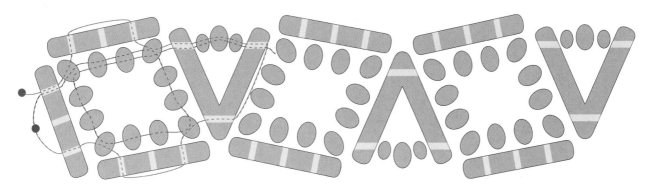

FIG. 1

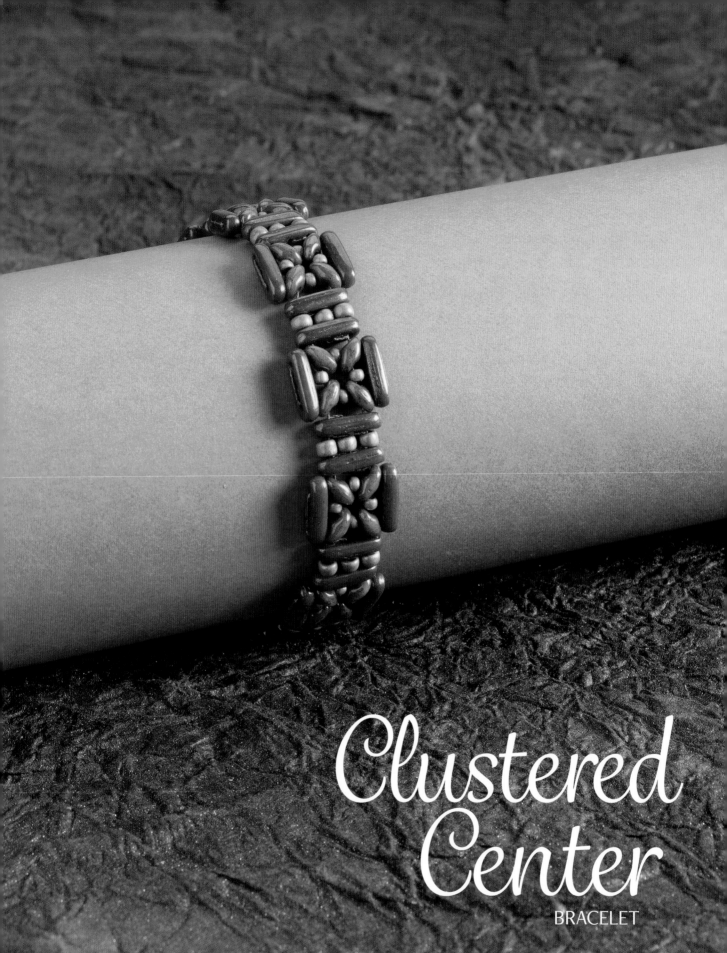

Clustered
Center
BRACELET

The cluster stitch is a kind of right-angle weave. The box of two- or three-hole beads is the same, but the interior uses SuperDuos in the corners of the box. Only a small change is needed to make this lovely piece.

supplies

7-in. (18cm) bracelet

- **42** three-hole beam beads
- **40** SuperDuo beads
- **1g** 8º seed beads
- **.5g** 11º seed beads
- **1** magnetic clasp
- #10 or #11 beading needle
- 10 lb. test Power Pro or similar

1 **[FIG. 1, red thread]** Thread a needle with a comfortable length of thread. Pick up a beam bead (through an end hole), a SuperDuo bead, and a beam (end hole), turn, and sew through the other end hole of the second beam. Pick up another SuperDuo and beam (end hole), turn, and sew through the other end hole of the beam you just picked up. Pick up a SuperDuo and a beam (end hole), and sew through the other end hole of the beam you just picked up. Pick up a SuperDuo, and sew through the empty end hole of the first beam you picked up.

2 **[FIG. 1, blue thread]** Sew through the original hole of the first beam, continue through the same hole of the next SuperDuo, turn, and sew through the other hole of that SuperDuo. Pick up an 11º seed bead, and sew through the empty hole of the next SuperDuo around the circle. Repeat this stitch twice. Pick up an 11º, and sew through the beads until you reach the second SuperDuo. Turn and sew through the other hole of that SuperDuo, and continue through the top hole of the third beam.

3 **[FIG. 1, blue thread]** Pick up an 8º and a beam (end hole), turn, and sew back into the center hole of the same beam. Pick up another 8º, and sew through the center hole of the adjacent beam. Turn and sew through the end hole of the same beam. Pick up an 8º, and sew through the empty hole of the new beam. Turn the work upside down to be in a position to continue making sections until you reach the desired length. Attach the clasp (see "Attaching clasps," p. 7). End the threads.

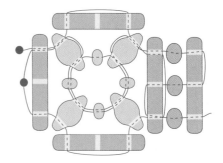

FIG. 1

Double and Triple
BRACELET

IRAW, like any other stitch, can be doubled and tripled and made to create a surface. When you have a textured surface that's the same all over, color is a great way to make it pop. I've chosen to use bars in a neutral color. Inside the boxes I've created some color contrast to the gray by using orange as a base and blending it with value-contrasting black and ivory to create an interesting pattern.

supplies

6⅜-in. (16.2cm) bracelet, not including clasp

- **160** two-hole bar beads
- **5g** 11º seed beads
- **1** 3-loop clasp
- #10 or #11 beading needle
- 10 lb. test Power Pro or similar

1 **[FIG. 1]** Thread a needle with a comfortable length of thread. Build the first row as in steps 1–3 of the "Splendid Singlet Bracelet," p. 78. Continue adding blocks until you reach the desired length. When you reach the end, you can go off in any of three directions. In this case, you will want to go either up or down in order to turn back and make an attached row. Remember, you can turn the work over if you like. It's the same on both sides. Continue building blocks as in the previous steps.

2 **[FIG. 2]** I prefer to go back into the work a bit in order strengthen the piece at the point of turning. You can retrace your thread around the entire block (including bars) or just around the center beads, then exit the last block in the first row where you want to start the new row. If you are confused about how to proceed, rotate the work so your starting point looks like the original one, with the first 11º seed bead in the upper left corner.

3 Continue the second row, incorporating the nearest bar of the first row as the lower bar in the second row. Work across the length of the bracelet. Turn again as in step 2 to make a third row. End the threads and attach the clasp (see "Attaching clasps," p. 7).

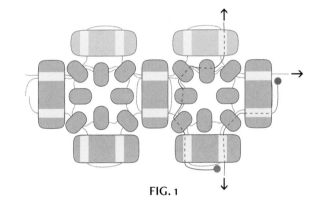

FIG. 1

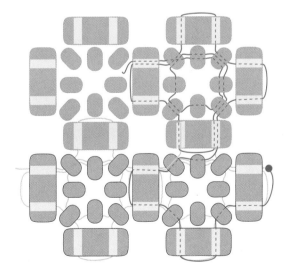

FIG. 2

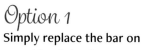

Option 1

Simply replace the bar on one side of the first row with a tile or stud, then use that tile or stud as the attaching bar for a second row.

Option 2

You could choose any mid-tone shade of blue or green or purple, and contrast it with a light and a dark in the same pattern. Or, try all black bars and all white seed beads, or the reverse. Try all the same color except for the seed beads in the middle row.

Zig-Zag

NECKLACE

Pretty on its own, this zig-zag pattern can form the base for a number of variations. Once you've learned to turn, as we did in the previous "Double and Triple Bracelet," p. 92, this should be an easy trick. Colors make the pattern in this IRAW design show up. I've used three colors: one is neutral (gray), and two are contrasting (orange and wine).

supplies

- **76** two-hole bar beads
- **2g** 11º seed beads (**1g** color A, **1g** color B)
- assorted beads that fit between the created blocks for embellishing and stringing
- **1** magnetic clasp
- #10 or #11 beading needle
- 10 lb. test Power Pro or similar

1 Now that you know how to turn, it's easy to make the single row into a three-block zig-zag shape. Once I have the zig-zag made, I like to start with a new thread in the center, adding beads that will fit between the upper points of the zig-zag and finishing the side strands with similar seed beads. Be sure that you don't pull the sections too tight or pack them so full that you distort the shape of the necklace. You will need a slight curve to fit around the front of the neck.

2 Take both threads out, stringing matching seed beads, to the length you need. String a clasp, turn around, and sew back into the work, tying knots as you go. End the threads.

Option 1
Start with a zig-zag necklace base and fill the spaces with a combination of Silky beads and seed beads. Add drops to each point and corner.

Option 3

Another easy option is to create free triangles of different sizes and attach them together on a strand. As with the other pieces, you can add feature beads, edging, or drops.

Option 2

Again, start with a zig-zag, using SuperDuos instead of bars and 15°s instead of 11° seed beads. Add edging all around with SuperDuos and drops on the points.

Geomancy
NECKLACE

One of my all-time favorite neck pieces, I've tried it in many colors and always had great results. The shape is flattering to most necklines and shows off what intricate beadwork you can do. Enlarge it. Add decorative beads along the lower edge as you turn to go back into the other hole of the bottom bar. Add some bead embroidery or an edging. I hope you enjoy it as much as I have.

supplies

- **10** two-hole tile beads
- **120+** two-hole bar beads
- **1g** 11º seed beads
- **2g** 8º seed beads (approximately) to finish the neck strand
- **10** large two-hole accent beads
- **1** clasp
- #10 or #11 beading needle
- 10 lb. test Power Pro or similar thread

1 Begin by making a simple zig-zag with five downward points, but with four blocks to a row instead of three.

2 **[FIG. 1, blue beads]** Add a second row along the bottom of the center three sections, being sure to increase using an additional bar and seed bead as shown in the blue beads in the illustration at the beginning and end of the new row.

3 Add a third row to the center section, again increasing at the beginning and end of the row.

4 **[FIG. 1, green beads]** With a new thread, join the top point using the tile beads and 8º and 11º seed beads.

5 String the side strands with matching beads, and attach a clasp (see "Attaching clasps," p. 7) Return to the center, and end the threads.

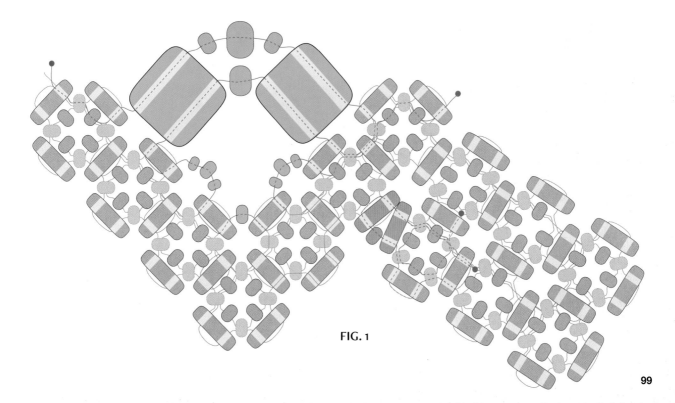

FIG. 1

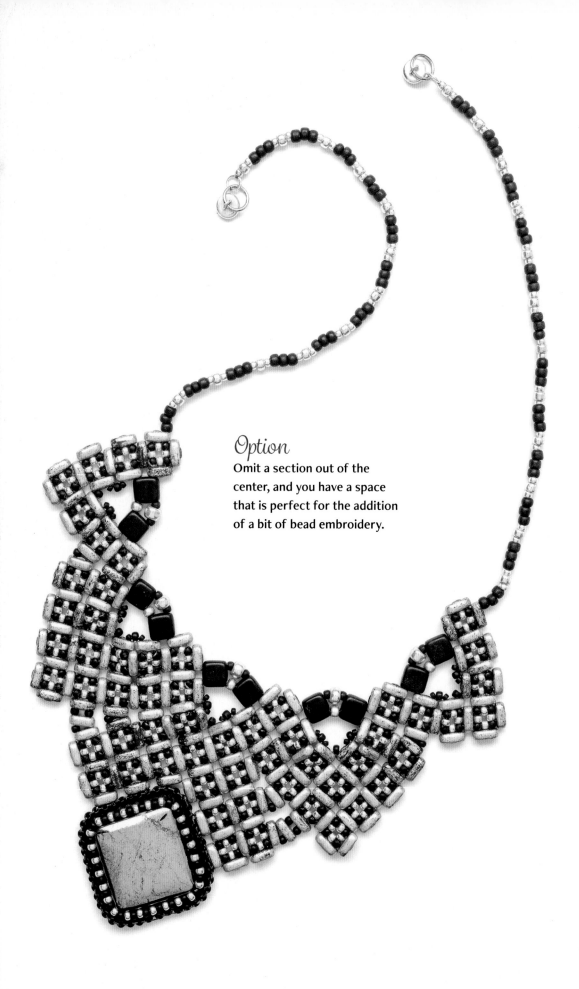

Option
Omit a section out of the center, and you have a space that is perfect for the addition of a bit of bead embroidery.

Off-Center

BRACELET

A bit of an unusual look, but captivating, is this use of only two of the holes of a three-hole beam bead. This technique is a bit tricky until you get used to the angles and understand which holes to use.

supplies

6-in (15.2cm) bracelet, not including clasp

- **72** three-hole beam beads
- **6g** 8° seed beads
- **1** 3-loop clasp
- #10 or #11 beading needle
- 10 lb. test Power Pro or similar

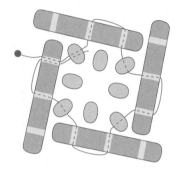

FIG. 1

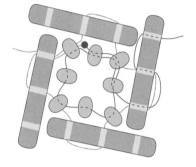

FIG. 2

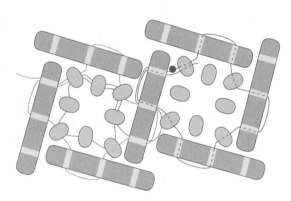

FIG. 3

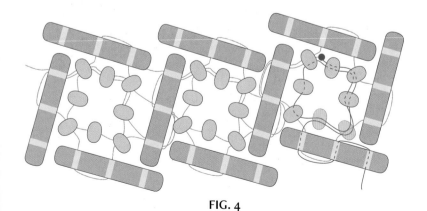

FIG. 4

1 **[FIG. 1, red thread]** Thread a needle on a comfortable length of thread. Pick up a beam bead (through an end hole), an 8° seed bead, and a beam (center hole), turn, and sew back through the end hole of the same beam. Pick up an 8° and a beam (center hole), turn, and sew through the end hole of the same beam. Pick up an 8° and a beam (center hole), turn, and sew through the end hole of the same beam. Pick up an 8°, and sew in through the center hole of the first beam. Turn and sew through the end hole where you started, and continue through the first 8°.

2 **[FIG. 2, blue thread]** Pick up an 8°, and sew through the adjacent 8° around the inner circle four times and exit the first 8°. Sew through the next two 8°s around the inner circle, continue out through the bottom hole of the rightmost beam, turn, sew through the center hole of the same beam, turn again, and sew out through the upper hole of the same beam.

3 **[FIG. 3]** Repeat steps 1–2 until you reach the desired length.

4 **[FIG. 4, blue thread]** In the last IRAW box, continue through two additional 8°s around the inner circle (orange beads), sew through the end hole, back through the center hole, and continue through the other end hole of the bottom beam, just as you did with the end beam.

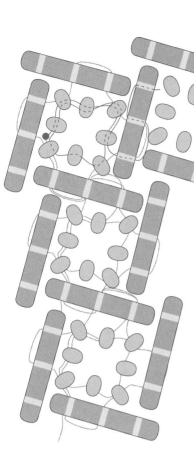

5 **[FIG. 5]** Rotate the end of the bracelet one turn to the left, and you will see that you are in position to build another IRAW box at a right angle to the end box. Do so.

6 **[FIG. 6, red and blue threads]** Continue to build IRAW boxes along the upper edge of the original row. The new beads are in orange and the green beads are the beams that join the new row to the original row. Repeat until you have finished that row. Attach a clasp (see "Attaching clasps," p. 7), and end the threads.

FIG. 5

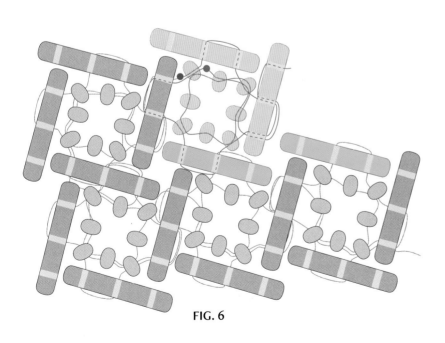

FIG. 6

Option
I've made a long line neckpiece using this technique. I created two segments and joined them together with round beads.

Cab and Cluster

BRACELET

Combining the off-center beam construction with the cluster center, and an alternating cabochon section, this bracelet has real charm and an Art Nouveau feel.

supplies

6½-in. (16.5cm) bracelet, not including clasp

- **28** three-hole beam beads
- **8** 8mm two-hole cabochons
- **28** SuperDuo beads
- **1.5g** 11º seed beads
- **1** 1 or 2-ring clasp
- **#10** or **#11** beading needle
- 10 lb. test Power Pro or similar thread

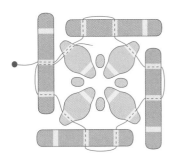

FIG. 1

1 [**FIG. 1, red thread**] Thread a needle on a comfortable length of thread. Pick up a beam bead (through a center hole), * a SuperDuo bead, and a beam (end hole), turn, and sew back through the center hole of the same beam. Pick up a SuperDuo and a beam (end hole), turn, and sew back through the center hole of the same beam. Pick up a SuperDuo and a beam (end hole), turn, and sew back through the center hole of the same beam. Pick up a SuperDuo, and sew through the bottom hole of the original beam. Turn and sew back through the center hole of that same beam, and continue through the same hole of the first SuperDuo.

2 [**FIG. 2, red thread**] Pick up an 11º seed bead, and sew through the empty hole of the next SuperDuo clockwise around the inner circle. Repeat three times, and exit the original 11º. Continue through the same holes of the next SuperDuo, 11º, and SuperDuo. Turn, and sew through the other hole of the SuperDuo you are exiting, and continue through the center hole of the rightmost beam.

3 [**FIG. 3, red thread**] Pick up an 11º, a two-hole cabochon (right hole), an 11º, and a beam (end hole), turn, and sew back through the center hole of the same beam. Pick up an 11º, sew through the other hole of the cab, pick up another 11º, and sew through the upper hole of the previous beam. Turn, sew through the center hole of the same beam, and continue through the 11º, cabochon, 11º, and bottom hole of the new beam. Turn and sew through the upper end hole of the same beam, turn again, and sew through the center hole of the same beam. Repeat from the * in step 1 to the desired length.

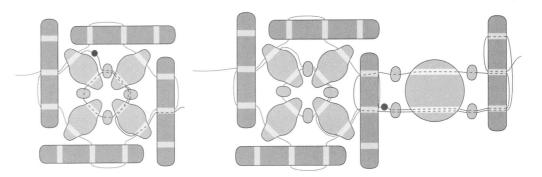

FIG. 2   FIG. 3

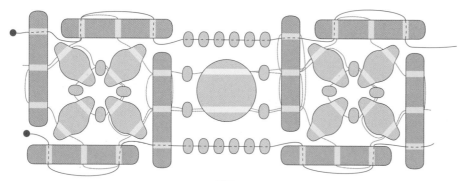

FIG. 4

4 **[FIG. 4, red threads]** You will need to make an edging along both sides of the bracelet. Sew through the beadwork to exit the upper hole of the end vertical beam. Turn and sew through the end hole of the next horizontal beam, then turn and sew through the other end hole. (Add beads to decorate the edging here, if desired.) Pick up six 11⁰s, and sew through the upper hole of the next vertical beam. Repeat until you have finished one side. Repeat this step on the other side of the bracelet.

5 **[FIG. 5, red thread]** You began the bracelet with an IRAW box, and if that fits with your length, you can simply attach a clasp there—but if you need more length or want a symmetrical piece, add a cabochon section to the original end. Add the clasp (see "Attaching clasps," p. 7), and end the threads.

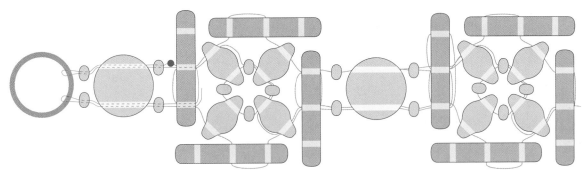

FIG. 5

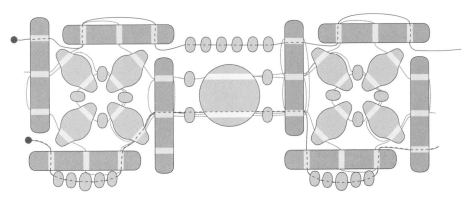

FIG. 6

Option

To turn the bracelet into a necklace, refer to **FIG. 6**. Along the top, work the same edging as the bracelet. On the bottom edge, skip the six 11°s and add beads only on the bottom edge of the lower beams. You can embellish the edge further by adding beads along the bottom of the beams.

This necklace is based on running
stitch. The pink cabochon just called
out to be added as a centerpiece.

Gallery

Another variation on the
S-Braid, this leafy look
makes a nice statment with
its Pyramid bead center.

Dice? Why not a pair for earrings?
Each side is numbered with black
matte seed beads. Or try a rainbow
of colors as dangles for a necklace or
charm bracelet.

Playing around with blue
AVA beads gave me the idea
for adding this beautiful
denim cabochon, and the
matching blue antique cab
beads made the perfect
addition.

S-Braid is so versatile, and color can be made to play a big part in the designs. This necklace fades from wine to pink and features hexagon beads instead of tile beads.

Acknowledgments

Thanks to Kalmbach for their confidence in me and my designs, and for their excellent editing, production, and promotion of all my books. Thanks also to the galleries who sell my work (you know who you are) and keep me in business.

Another variation on IRAW using par Puca Tinos beads. The blocks of IRAW translate easily into matching earrings, and a par Puca Kheops bead is used to attach the earring back.

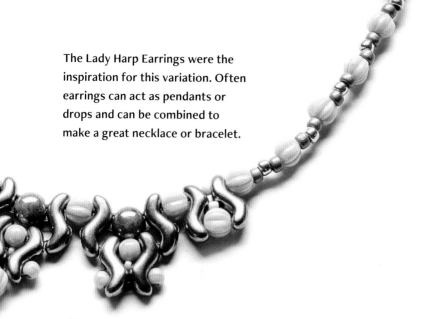

The Lady Harp Earrings were the inspiration for this variation. Often earrings can act as pendants or drops and can be combined to make a great necklace or bracelet.

From the Author

Still no bead store in my hometown! I feel quite neglected. But the internet makes a delightfully bigger world for all of us beaders living in small towns. We only need the patience to wait a few days. And I'm encouraged to make that special trip to Denver or Albuquerque, or to the nearest bead show.

As a "lonely" beader, I appreciate most of all the inspiration that comes through bead magazines, such as *Bead&Button*, blogs, and Facebook. Two-hole beads seem to spur more and more online activity, partly because of their novelty, but mainly because they have opened so many avenues of creativity. As a designer, it's both inspiring to see what other designers are doing, and a bit overwhelming to see so many great designs flowing from all over the world.

In my observation of the design process, I've realized that much of what a bead designer does is make all the mistakes first so you don't have to. I may remake a piece seven or eight times before the right beads, the right path, and the right drape become clear. Even then, the color may not be right. Or I'll notice something on my work table that prompts further exploration. Or remember a bead I bought a year or two ago that's been waiting for its place.

Every designer has her own process. Most of my designs grow out of previous exploration. And I have my own preferences. I see many round pieces—rosettes, balls, cameos, cabochon settings, and such. They don't challenge me. I love a good stitch I can sink my teeth into. Make it play and grow and expand into pattern and shape. That is the desire that motivated the sections on S-Braid and IRAW. I would love to see beaders get into these stitches and design pieces of their own because of the new avenues that S-Braid and IRAW offer.

When I'm not beading, I'm working with my local Art Jewelry group or on the board of the regional writer's association in Western Colorado. I love to write poetry and short stories, and I have a couple of unpublished novels under my belt. I spend a lot of time with my nose in a book. I'm currently working more in combining bead weaving with bead embroidery. Check out my website, virjenmettle.com, to see what I'm currently up to.

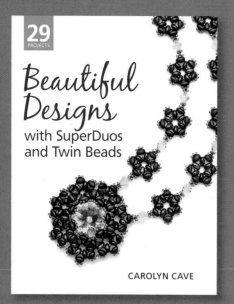

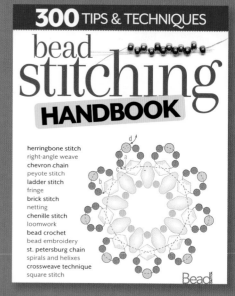